Praise for *Money for the Rest of Us*

"One of the biggest pitfalls in any decision we make is thinking we know more than we do. In *Money for the Rest of Us*, David Stein provides investors a framework that focuses attention on what we don't know, reduces overconfidence, and highlights the value of considering where things might go wrong. This is a high-impact framework for making any decision, not just investing."

—ANNIE DUKE, decision strategist and
bestselling author of *Thinking in Bets*

"David provides a clear road map for investors, brought to life through a series of personal anecdotes. He recognizes that past is not prologue, that the successful strategies of recent years may not fare as well in the years ahead."

—ROB ARNOTT, Chairman, Research Affiliates

"You don't need to be a math whiz or financial expert to be a successful investor. Instead, you need a disciplined investment process, a framework that you can use to provide peace of mind when others are freaking out. The most honest and successful investors have no more idea about what is going to happen in the future than you or I do. What makes them different? They have an investment philosophy and decision-making process that directs their investment choices. Stein gives us the best framework I've seen for easily evaluating the most important aspects of any investment so you can accomplish your personal finance goals."

—MICHAEL PORT, *New York Times* and *Wall Street Journal*
bestselling author of seven books including *Steal the Show*
and *Book Yourself Solid*

"They say you should write the book you want to read; with *Money for the Rest of Us*, David has gone one better. He's written the book he knows his audience wants to read because he's spent years understanding their needs and addressing their unanswered questions. David doesn't want to tell people how to invest—he wants to help people to have the confidence to make smart investment decisions for themselves. If you are one of those people, then this book is for you."

—BERNADETTE JIWA, bestselling author,
Australian top business thinker

"We all have 50 questions about investing. David Stein proves what a great teacher he is by distilling the list to *the* 10 you really need to know. Whether you're investing to grow your nest egg or to protect it, there's something here for everyone. A must read."

—JOE SAUL-SEHY, creator and cohost of
Stacking Benjamins podcast

"If you want to be a successful investor, *Money for the Rest of Us* should be a marked-up resource sitting on your desk. David Stein presents a valuable outline for making better investing decisions."

—ROGER P. WHITNEY, CFP®, CIMA®, CPWA®, RMA®, AIF,
and Retirement Answer Man

"David Stein's *Money for the Rest of Us* is a superb and accessible guide to investing. He gets right to the point and provides the reader with answers to the most pertinent questions we all have when trying to navigate the investment landscape. This book is a valuable addition to anyone's library."

—CULLEN ROCHE, founder of Orcam Financial Group
and author of *Pragmatic Capitalism*

MONE
FOR THE
REST OF L

Praise for *Money for the Rest of Us*

"One of the biggest pitfalls in any decision we make is thinking we know more than we do. In *Money for the Rest of Us*, David Stein provides investors a framework that focuses attention on what we don't know, reduces overconfidence, and highlights the value of considering where things might go wrong. This is a high-impact framework for making any decision, not just investing."

—ANNIE DUKE, decision strategist and
bestselling author of *Thinking in Bets*

"David provides a clear road map for investors, brought to life through a series of personal anecdotes. He recognizes that past is not prologue, that the successful strategies of recent years may not fare as well in the years ahead."

—ROB ARNOTT, Chairman, Research Affiliates

"You don't need to be a math whiz or financial expert to be a successful investor. Instead, you need a disciplined investment process, a framework that you can use to provide peace of mind when others are freaking out. The most honest and successful investors have no more idea about what is going to happen in the future than you or I do. What makes them different? They have an investment philosophy and decision-making process that directs their investment choices. Stein gives us the best framework I've seen for easily evaluating the most important aspects of any investment so you can accomplish your personal finance goals."

—MICHAEL PORT, *New York Times* and *Wall Street Journal*
bestselling author of seven books including *Steal the Show*
and *Book Yourself Solid*

"They say you should write the book you want to read; with *Money for the Rest of Us*, David has gone one better. He's written the book he knows his audience wants to read because he's spent years understanding their needs and addressing their unanswered questions. David doesn't want to tell people how to invest—he wants to help people to have the confidence to make smart investment decisions for themselves. If you are one of those people, then this book is for you."

—BERNADETTE JIWA, bestselling author,

Australian top business thinker

"We all have 50 questions about investing. David Stein proves what a great teacher he is by distilling the list to *the* 10 you really need to know. Whether you're investing to grow your nest egg or to protect it, there's something here for everyone. A must read."

—JOE SAUL-SEHY, creator and cohost of

Stacking Benjamins podcast

"If you want to be a successful investor, *Money for the Rest of Us* should be a marked-up resource sitting on your desk. David Stein presents a valuable outline for making better investing decisions."

—ROGER P. WHITNEY, CFP®, CIMA®, CPWA®, RMA®, AIF,

and Retirement Answer Man

"David Stein's *Money for the Rest of Us* is a superb and accessible guide to investing. He gets right to the point and provides the reader with answers to the most pertinent questions we all have when trying to navigate the investment landscape. This book is a valuable addition to anyone's library."

—CULLEN ROCHE, founder of Orcam Financial Group

and author of *Pragmatic Capitalism*

MONEY

FOR THE

REST OF US

Contents

Acknowledgments

Thanks to Bernadette Jiwa for coming up with the *Money for the Rest of Us* book title and to my agent Paul Lucas for the motivation to write the book four years after I had a title. To my editor, Noah Schwartzberg, for believing in and supporting the project. To my sons, Bret and Camden, for your countless hours of editing help. To the tens of thousands of *Money For the Rest of Us* podcast listeners for your support, questions, and ideas. To the 1,000 Money For the Rest of Us Plus members for being there as we help each other on our respective financial journeys. Special thanks to Plus members who served as early readers for the candid feedback that made for a better book: Catherine Anderson, Kent Baggett, Justin Belk, James Blandford, Robin Crisler, Marc DuVal, Christopher Ellis, Peter Forint, Simon Gogolin, Greg Golich, Anthony Indovina, Julia Khanova, Paul LaFrance, Mick Parent, Joseph Pelusi, Kathleen Pritchard, Michael Reese, Joe Talbert, David Toberisky, Dr. Alexander Walkhoff, Matt Weiser, and one member who chose to remain anonymous.

Introduction

THE TEN QUESTIONS

1. What is it?

2. Is it investing, speculating, or gambling?

3. What is the upside?

4. What is the downside?

5. Who is on the other side of the trade?

6. What is the investment vehicle?

7. What does it take to be successful?

8. Who is getting a cut?

9. How does it impact your portfolio?

10. Should you invest?

Several years ago, I met an exterminator at our farm in Teton Valley, Idaho. The 80-acre investment property and vacation home has sweeping views of barley fields and the Teton mountain range. Elk and moose frequent the land, and mountain bluebirds flit from tree to tree.

Our dream property had two problems. The first was a mice infestation in the house. Hence, the exterminator. The second problem was more serious. Across the road and down a bit from our farm, an abandoned gravel pit that had sat idle for almost a decade was again in full operation. Every few minutes, a dump truck loaded with gravel drove past our house, stirring up dust. The silence that attracted us to this beautiful spot was broken. A rock crusher operated at the gravel pit 12 hours a day. The great bargain we thought we got when we purchased the farm at the bottom of the housing collapse no longer seemed so attractive.

The exterminator and I chatted as he placed bait boxes around the house. I mentioned to him I used to be an institutional investment advisor and now taught individuals about money, investing, and the economy on my podcast and membership community.

He turned to me and asked, "How much can someone earn per year investing in stocks?"

Before I could reply, he answered his own question. "I think 80% is reasonable."

It turns out he had bought his first stock earlier that year, and it had appreciated over 80%. That was the rate of return that now anchored his expectations. He was unpersuaded by my attempt to explain what determined stock returns and why his expectations were off by a factor of 10.

MAKING INVESTMENT MISTAKES IS NORMAL

The exterminator and I both made investment mistakes. His was he didn't really understand how stocks worked, so his expectations were unrealistic; and mine was falling in love with a piece of real estate without adequately researching the status of the nearby gravel pit. Making investing mistakes is normal. All investors, even highly successful hedge funds, make mistakes. Ned Davis, a renowned investor and market technician, said: "We are in the business of making mistakes. The only difference between the winners and the losers is that the winners make small mistakes, while the losers make big mistakes."[1]

As individuals saving and investing for retirement, we need to get comfortable with the fact we will make some mistakes. We can't let the fear of doing so keep us from investing. At the same time, we can't afford to make big investment mistakes. Being a loser in that realm means running out of money during retirement or not being able to retire at all. Over my investment career, I've interviewed hundreds of money managers, including stock investors, bond managers, hedge funds, and venture capitalists, in order to understand how they invest. I always asked them to give me an example of an investment mistake they made and what they learned from it. Not only have I learned from other investors' mistakes, but I have also learned from my own. I advised and made financial recommendations to dozens of endowments and foundations with billions of dollars of assets. Some of my recommendations worked out, while others were mistakes. As Chief Portfolio and Investment Strategist, I also had day-to-day responsibility for managing a $2 billion investment portfolio, guiding it through the 2008 global financial crisis with clients and partners evaluating and critiquing every portfolio move, including my mistakes.

Warren Buffett, one of the most successful investors ever, has said we beat ourselves up too much over our mistakes.[2] Yet we all do it. I remember my investment mistakes way more than I remember my successes. One reason we are so hard on ourselves about our mistakes is we have a difficult time separating a bad outcome from the decision-making process.

Professional poker player and decision-making specialist Annie Duke, in her book *Thinking in Bets: Making Smarter Decisions When You Don't Have All the Facts*, wrote: "What makes a decision great is not that it has a great outcome. A great decision is the result of a good process. . . . Decisions are bets on the future, and they aren't right or wrong based on whether they turn out well on any particular iteration. An unwanted result doesn't make our decisions wrong if we thought about the alternatives and probabilities in advance and allocated our resources according-ly."[3] Sometimes investments don't work out as expected, but that does not mean it was a mistake if the decision was well thought out. We have to take what we can learn from the experience and move on to the next investment opportunity.

YOU ARE A PORTFOLIO MANAGER

When it comes to investing, you and I are portfolio managers. Portfolio managers compare different investment opportunities and allocate money among them. A key aim of this book is to teach you a framework, a good process, for making those allocation decisions so that even if there is an occasional bad outcome, the impact on your financial livelihood is small. In the face of extreme uncertainty, a disciplined investment process can give you confidence and peace of mind when others are overwhelmed with the number of financial choices or panicking during the latest market sell-off. An investment discipline can help you overcome the fear of making mistakes while avoiding large ones.

A DIFFERENT KIND OF INVESTING BOOK

I no longer manage money professionally. Now my biggest financial challenge is the same as yours: making sure I have enough money to retire and that those resources last. For the past five years, I've hosted one of the world's most popular investment podcasts, *Money For the Rest of Us*. Listeners often ask if there is a book I can recommend that will teach them how to invest. There are, of course, a lot of investing books. Many are for beginners, walking readers through the steps of opening up a brokerage account, explaining what an index fund is, and discussing why it is important to save and diversify. Other investment books get into the nitty-gritty details of trying to beat the stock market by employing value investing or momentum strategies, trading options or foreign currencies, or building a portfolio of real estate investments.

This book is different. Although it includes plenty of information on various investment strategies, its main goal is to take a step back and show you how to evaluate investment opportunities so that you can decide whether you should even be trading options, building out a real estate portfolio, or trying to beat the stock market by investing like Warren Buffett. This book is organized into a ten-question framework for analyzing any investment, so you can avoid big mistakes and increase your odds at profiting from successful investments no matter what they are. In short, this book is for investors who are portfolio and asset class focused, who have demonstrated the discipline to save and invest for retirement, and who want to make sure they are doing everything they can to confidently protect and grow their wealth.

WHAT YOU WILL LEARN

The truth is you don't need to be an expert to be a successful investor. We are able to navigate many complex domains without being an expert. These domains include managing our homes and businesses, traveling the world, and playing a sport. We navigate complexity through rules of thumb: heuristics that guide our actions. In this book I share rules of thumb to guide your investment decisions.

You will learn about the answers to these questions:

- What is the difference between investing, speculating, and gambling?
- How do you determine an investment's expected return, its potential upside, and its potential downside?
- What is required to beat the stock market, and should you try?
- How do you build a diversified portfolio without getting bogged down in the minutiae of modern portfolio theory?

- What is the difference between exchange-traded funds (ETFs), mutual funds, and closed-end funds, and what are the risks of each?
- Does using passive index funds mean you should be passive in all areas of your investing?
- Is it better to invest a lump sum all at once or to dollar-cost average?
- Should you own gold or cryptocurrencies, and should you trade foreign currencies?
- Should you pursue dividend investing or invest outside your home country?

And much, much more.

This book is designed to be approachable and helpful to both beginners and those that have been investing on their own for years. It is a book that you can feel good about sharing with others, and I would be honored if you would do so. Many of the quotes I have included in this book are from investment mentors. Some I have met in person, but most I have not. These are virtual mentors, individuals whose approach to investing and managing risk I have followed and admired for years. I have included these quotes not only to reinforce the book's core principles but also to serve as a reminder of how much we can learn about investing from the experience of others.

I don't know how my exterminator's stock portfolio is doing, but our investment in our Teton Valley farm worked out despite the gravel pit. We split the property into two 40-acre parcels and sold the parcel with the house, pastures, barn, and other outbuildings to a woman who is operating it as an overnight camp and retreat center for those that want to work with horses and experience living on a ranch. We will more than likely sell her the remaining 40 acres as her new enterprise becomes more established. We broke even on the investment financially, and if we factor in the wonderful experiences we had with family and friends on the property, then we came out well ahead.

1
What Is It?

*If We Can't Explain an Investment,
Then We Shouldn't Invest*

THE TEN QUESTIONS

1. **What is it?**
2. Is it investing, speculating, or gambling?
3. What is the upside?
4. What is the downside?
5. Who is on the other side of the trade?
6. What is the investment vehicle?
7. What does it take to be successful?
8. Who is getting a cut?
9. How does it impact your portfolio?
10. Should you invest?

QUESTION ONE: WHAT IS IT?

Before we invest, we should seek to understand and explain in simple terms an investment's characteristics. The act of explaining keeps us humble and helps us realize what we don't know. Answering the ten questions discussed in this book forms an investment discipline that can give us confidence in the face of uncertainty.

Do you remember your first stock investment? I bought my first stock when I was in graduate school getting an MBA with an emphasis in finance. The stock was Novell. Every night after school, I watched the *Nightly Business Report* on PBS to see how the stock performed that day. This was 1991, so it was several years before you could browse the web to get instant access to stock quotes.

Several years earlier, I had worked for a subsidiary of Novell as a temp employee while living in Provo, Utah. My job consisted of assembling the instruction manuals for Netware, Novell's leading product.

Peter Lynch, the renowned mutual fund manager, is famous for his advice, "Invest in what you know."[1] I knew Novell. Well, I at least knew of it. I had worked there, after all.

Later, Lynch clarified what he meant: "I've never said, 'If you go to a mall, see a Starbucks and say it's good coffee, you should call Fidelity brokerage and buy the stock. . . .' People buy a stock and they know nothing about it. . . . That's gambling and it's not good."[2]

My investment thesis for buying Novell was I thought the stock would go up because it did something with computer networking—what, exactly, I wasn't sure—and computers were getting ever more popular. I did no research on the company. I knew nothing about the industry or what was going on with the economy. I had no idea whether the stock was expensive or cheap. I simply took $1,000, about 25% of my wife's and my life savings, and bought it, because I thought it would go up. In short, I gambled.

Buying Novell's stock would be the first, but not the last, time I invested in something because I thought it would go up in price without stopping to consider why. Clearly, a stock rises in price because other investors are willing to pay more. But why are they willing to pay more? For example, on September 17, 2017, the stock of Camping World, a retailer of recreation vehicles, jumped over 7%. What changed that would explain why investors collectively were willing to transact for Camping World's stock at a 7% higher price on a day when the overall U.S. stock market rose 0.3%? It turns out that Camping World's chief executive officer was interviewed on CNBC to provide more clarity on the company's strategy regarding recent acquisitions. He also said he had personally bought more of the company's stock.[3] After his remarks, investors collectively decided the price of Camping World's stock was wrong, and its correct price should be 7% higher.

Financial theory states that the correct price of a stock is the value in today's dollars of a company's future cash flow in terms of the share of the profits it pays to the shareholders, the owners of the stock. That percentage of profits distributed to shareholders is called a dividend. The value today of those future dividends per share of stock is known as the present value or intrinsic value. The correct price of a stock share should equal the present value of that dividend stream. Another way to think about present value is that it is the value that makes an investor indifferent to receiving cash today or cash in the future. We will explore present value in more detail in Chapter 4. One challenge with investing is no one knows for sure what the right price is for a stock because no one knows what the future dividends will be. In addition, some stocks don't currently pay dividends and won't for many years into the future.

THE PRIMARY REASON TO BUY
AN INDIVIDUAL STOCK

Here, then, is the most important principle I know when it comes to stock investing: The primary reason to buy an individual stock rather than a basket of stocks via an index mutual fund or exchange-traded fund (ETF) is if you believe the current stock price is too low. We don't buy a stock because we think the company will grow fast or because it has cool products, as I did with Novell. We primarily buy a stock because we believe other investors are wrong. That they have underestimated what the company's future profit and dividend growth will be. That the present value of future dividends per share is higher than the current share price. Why? Because the stock will only go up in price if the company does better than the consensus view. In other words, if the company surprises to the upside.

I seldom buy individual stocks, which are also known as equities, because I'm not willing to spend the time researching them to determine if investors are wrong and the stock is mispriced. Fortunately, in the case of Novell, I got lucky and the stock appreciated. I sold it a year or so later to help fund the down payment on our first home.

My investment in Novell's stock epitomizes how *not* to invest. Had I asked myself the ten questions detailed in this book that we should all ask when considering a new investment, I never would have bought the stock. And I wouldn't have even needed to ask myself ten questions. Simply asking the first question, "What is it?" would have helped me realize I didn't know what I was doing.

IF YOU CAN'T EXPLAIN IT, DON'T INVEST

One of my first investment advisory clients was a liberal arts college in Indiana. At one of our meetings, the chair of the college's investment committee said to me, "If I can't explain an investment we are considering to another board member who isn't on the committee, then we shouldn't invest." That is one of the most helpful pieces of investment advice I have ever received.

I definitely couldn't explain what Novell's business was when I invested or why its stock was priced too low. But my naivety went beyond that. I didn't even have a good understanding of where my money was going or who had sold me the stock.

When I invested in Novell, I bought the stock through my broker, who facilitated the trade on the Nasdaq stock exchange. Novell never saw the money. My money went to whomever sold me the stock. The stock traded in what is known as the secondary market. The only time a company gets money for a stock is when the company issues new stock shares as part of an initial public offering or a secondary offering. Once those shares are issued and the company collects the proceeds, then the shares trade among investors in the secondary market.

WHO IS SELLING IT?

If Novell wasn't selling me the stock, then in my quest to understand the investment, I should have stopped to consider who was selling the stock to me and why? We often do that when we buy a house or a used car. Knowing why someone is selling a house or a car is important information that helps us negotiate the price. If we know the seller is highly motivated to get rid of an item, our initial offer might be less than if the seller seemed ambivalent about closing a sale.

Of course, there is a brokerage firm that stands between us and the seller when we buy a stock, so we never know exactly who is selling the shares to us. Yet knowing the type of entities that dominate trading in a particular asset category is critical to deciding if and how we want to participate.

In 1952, three years after the renowned investor Benjamin Graham published *The Intelligent Investor*, his classic book on value investing, 75% of stocks were held directly by households.[4] That meant when Benjamin Graham bought a stock in 1952, he knew much more about it than the household selling it. He had an informational edge that allowed him to determine the stock was mispriced, and he was rewarded with outsized returns.

By the time I bought Novell in 1991, 42% of stocks were held directly by households.[5] Pension plans, insurance companies, and mutual funds were significant players in the stock market. Many of those pension plans and insurance companies hired outside money managers to manage portfolios for them. In other words, there was a professional class of investors who spent hour upon hour researching companies and valuing stocks. In that environment, it was unlikely I would have any type of informational edge compared with the seller to determine if Novell's stock was priced too low, even if I had done some preliminary research. Now markets have changed again, and when you buy a stock, it is most likely an institution's computer algorithm that sold it to you.

WE MAY NOT KNOW AS MUCH AS WE THINK

When considering a new investment, we should first ask, "What is it?"

We should be able to explain in simple terms where the money is going, who is selling it to us, and how the money will be used to generate a positive return. Similar to my former client, if we are unable to explain the investment to a family member or friend in a way that the person can understand, then we shouldn't invest.

In 2017, there was a mania surrounding cryptocurrencies such as Bitcoin. That year the price of Bitcoin went from less than $1,000 per coin to over $19,000. Many investors around the world began investing in Bitcoin for the first time. I am convinced that most of the new Bitcoin buyers if asked, "What is it?" would have been unable to explain in detail what Bitcoin is and how it works.

There is a critical reason why we need to be able to answer, "What is it?" before we invest. The simple act of trying to explain an investment keeps us humble and helps us realize what we don't know. Cognitive scientists Frank Keil and Leon Rozenblit conducted numerous studies asking people to explain how something as simple as a zipper worked. They found that as individuals tried to verbalize what they knew about a topic, they soon realized they didn't know as much as they thought. The exercise of explaining humbled them.[6] The fear of missing out on a hot opportunity like Bitcoin often leads us to be overconfident—we are convinced that we know more than we actually do. By pausing to answer, "What is it?" in as much detail as possible, we can see where we have gaps in our understanding and seek to fill them.

DEALING WITH UNKNOWNS

Ray Dalio, founder of the hedge fund Bridgewater Associates and one of the world's most successful investors, wrote, "Whatever success I've had in life has had more to do with my knowing how to deal with my *not* knowing than anything I know."[7] As we seek to explain what an investment is, we will find there are some things about the investment that are unknowable. One reason there are so many unknowns when it comes to investing is because financial markets are a nonlinear complex adaptive system. Let me explain what that is with the following anecdote.

Several years ago, I saw an approaching summer thunderstorm as I drove toward my home in southeastern Idaho. The storm didn't look terribly menacing. There were a few cumulonimbus clouds overhead, the type that pass through that time of year and sometimes bring rain and sometimes don't. Only this time the clouds stalled over my town, dropping two inches of rain in less than an hour—almost 15% of our annual rainfall with one storm. Flooding ensued. Canals overflowed. Streets became rivers. Basements were inundated with water.

The storm's severity was completely unexpected. The weather bureau didn't predict it. It was also very localized. A few miles north and south of my home it didn't rain at all. Thunderstorms are an example of a nonlinear system, which is a system that does not produce the same result every time, even though the inputs and conditions are the same.

Another example of nonlinearity is a pile of sand. If sand is dropped from above one grain at a time, it will create a cone-shaped pile that seems relatively stable. At some point, though, a grain of sand will hit the pile and trigger an avalanche. You would think the quantity of sand in the pile would be roughly the same each time an avalanche starts, but that is not the case. An avalanche can be triggered with only a few hundred grains of sand or thousands. The timing of an avalanche is not a function of the size of the pile but the dynamic interaction among the grains of sand—how they shift and slide relative to each other—their interdependence. The more grains of sand, the more interactions and the more difficult it becomes to predict when an avalanche will occur.[8]

COMPLEX ADAPTIVE SYSTEMS

Financial markets, like piles of sand and thunderstorms, are also nonlinear. They are a special class of nonlinearity called a complex adaptive system. Unlike a sand pile that is composed solely of sand, a complex adaptive system is composed of a wide variety of interconnected inputs that adapt and learn over time. There are millions of individual agents, both human and computer, that make up the financial markets, each striving to interpret ream upon ream of data about the economy, politics, business, technology, and human nature. Since market inputs are diverse and adapt over time, the interactions are even more complex than those found within a sand pile, making it impossible to predict when the next market avalanche will occur. It could be this year, or it could be in five.

Now just because we can't accurately predict when a huge market sell-off will occur doesn't mean we invest blindly. Even though weather forecasters couldn't predict that a storm would come to a standstill and deluge my town, meteorologists knew enough about atmospheric conditions to estimate that there was a higher risk of a thunderstorm in my area that day than on a typical day. And when the severity of the storm became apparent, they issued a warning so people could take cover. In other words, meteorologists reacted to the information they had.

REACTING TO AVAILABLE INFORMATION

If we invest in something without seeking to understand its characteristics, then that is like embarking on a lengthy wilderness expedition while ignoring everything that could be known about the climate, weather conditions, and terrain where we will be hiking. Doing so is reckless. When Ray Dalio says his success has more to do with knowing how to deal with his "not knowing,"[9] that does not mean he doesn't spend a great deal of time learning what can be known. Dalio says he loves to find people who disagree with him so he can see through their eyes what he might be missing. One of his favorite quotes is, "He who lives by the crystal ball is destined to eat ground glass." He then went on to say, "I had eaten enough glass to realize that what was most important wasn't knowing the future—it was knowing how to react appropriately to the information available at each point in time."[10]

Accurately forecasting the future is extremely difficult. In the year 1900, John Elfreth Watkins, Jr., published an article in *Ladies Home Journal* titled, "What May Happen in the Next Hundred Years." He envisioned a world in the year 2000 where strawberries were as big as apples and peas were as large as beets. A world where mosquitoes, flies, and roaches had been exterminated and horses were nearly extinct. A land where packages were delivered through a network of pneumatic tubes and the letters *C, X,* and *Q* had been eliminated from the everyday English alphabet in order to simplify it.[11]

Most of his predictions were wrong, although some were correct. Watkins correctly predicted wireless telephones and the television.[12] Imagine trying to pick investments based on those predictions. Even if you believed a television was possible, which company would you invest in? Which television manufacturer would survive? Which television company stock was mispriced because investors were underestimating the company's future dividends?

WHY ACCURATELY PREDICTING THE FUTURE IS SO DIFFICULT

Investing would be easy if we could accurately see the future. But we can't. Our imagined details are heavily influenced by our present attitudes, feelings, and knowledge. Most predictions end up being an extrapolation of current trends. We view the future through the lens of the present. What gets left out of predictions is the unpredictable—the unexpected events and surprises. It is these surprises that often have the greatest impact on the future. They are the game changers that can swamp the incremental improvements and current trends. As predictions become more detailed, there are a lot more surprises that could upend those predictions. That's another reason I rarely invest in individual stocks. I find that when I make specific predictions about what will happen to a company, usually something happens that I hadn't even considered.

There is a better way. As individual investors, if we don't have any particular insight about whether a specific stock is priced correctly or not, we can instead own baskets of hundreds, if not thousands, of stocks via a commingled investment vehicle such as an index mutual fund or ETF. That way we can benefit from positive surprises that drive up stock market prices without having to predict what those surprises will be.

Stocks are an example of a security, a tradable financial instrument in which an investor has an ownership right. A basket or group of securities with similar characteristics is known as an asset class. As individual investors, we are more likely to be successful if we focus on asset classes rather than individual securities. We can invest in asset classes through exchange-traded funds and mutual funds that are sponsored and managed by professional investment advisor teams.

INVESTING ON THE LEADING EDGE OF THE PRESENT

Ned Davis, who has more than 50 years of investment experience, recounted how his stock forecasts had been so good that in 1978 Louis Rukeyser, host of the *Wall Street Week* broadcast, said, "'Ned Davis has had an outstanding record in recent years . . . and has been absolutely right about most of the major ups and downs.'"[13]

Yet Ned Davis found that at the end of each year he hadn't made much money. He wrote:

> Before someone else could question me, I asked myself, "If you are so smart, why aren't you rich?" It was about that time (1978–1980) that I began to realize that smarts, hard work, and even a burning desire to be right were really not my problems, or the solution to my problems. My real problems were a failure to cut losses short, a lack of discipline and risk management, letting my ego color my market view (which made it difficult to admit mistakes), and difficulty controlling fear and greed. It was thus a lack of proper investment strategy and good money management techniques, not poor forecasting, that was holding me back.[14]

By investment strategy and risk management, Davis is referring to the same process Ray Dalio described: "React appropriately to the information available at each point in time."[15] I call this investing on the leading edge of the present. Answering the questions I share in this book before you invest in a new opportunity will give you critical information to act appropriately, even in the face of many unknowns.

THE MATH AND EMOTION OF INVESTING

When considering an investment opportunity, we need to understand the math and the emotion. By math I mean understanding the mechanics of what drives the returns of a particular investment: How bond returns are primarily driven by current interest rate yields. How stock returns are driven by dividend and corporate profit growth. How real estate returns are driven by rents. In other words, the math of investing involves understanding how a particular security or asset class generates cash flow. Business owners and potential buyers do the same thing as they assess how a business generates cash flow.

The emotion of investing is about understanding how investors are valuing investment cash flows. When investors place a high value on investment cash flows, bidding up security prices, then subsequent returns will be lower. When investors are fearful and place a low value on an investment's expected cash flow, then subsequent returns will be higher. Why will returns be higher? Because when an asset class's valuation is lower than normal and investors are pessimistic, there is a greater likelihood that individual securities in that basket will surprise to the upside. The asset class is embedded with future positive surprises. On the flip side, there is a greater likelihood for negative surprises when purchasing a basket of richly valued securities that is priced for perfection.

Knowing the math and emotion surrounding an asset class at a given point in time is like being the meteorologists who knew conditions were ripe for a thunderstorm on that summer day when my Idaho town was deluged, even if they didn't know exactly where a storm might hit. Knowing the math and emotion of an asset class, what I call investment conditions, is investing on the leading edge of the present. Of course, a critical aspect of investing is controlling our own emotions. We can't get caught up in the hype and fear that drives other investors into a frenzy or panic.

AN INVESTING FRAMEWORK

When we are first exposed to a new investment opportunity, we are often unable to answer the question, "What is it?" We have to figure out what it is by using the remaining nine questions I discuss in this book. These questions help us determine the math and the emotion surrounding the specific investment opportunity. We will come to know how the returns are generated, how investor emotions are influencing the expected returns, what is the downside, what are the fees, what is the investment vehicle, what are the tax consequences, and what has to happen for the investment to be successful. In addition, answering these questions helps us realize the limit of our understanding. That there is much we don't know. Not knowing helps us to not become overconfident and make big investment mistakes. Collectively, these questions form an investment discipline that can gives us confidence in the face of uncertainty.

CHAPTER SUMMARY

- When considering a new investment, we should first ask, "What is it?" We should be able to explain in simple terms where the money is going, who is selling it to us, and how the money will be used to generate a positive return.

- If we don't have any particular insight about whether a specific stock is priced correctly or not, then it is better to own baskets of hundreds, if not thousands, of stocks via commingled investment vehicles like index mutual funds or ETFs.

- The act of trying to explain an investment keeps us humble and helps us realize what we don't know and what can't be known.

- If we are unable to explain an investment to a family member or friend in a way that the person can understand, then we shouldn't invest.

- Knowledge about the math and the emotion surrounding an investment helps us do the right thing at the right time while avoiding mistakes.

- The math of investing involves understanding how a particular security or asset class generates cash flow. The emotion of investing is about understanding how investors are valuing those investment cash flows.

2

Is It Investing, Speculating, or Gambling?

A Simple Filter for Segmenting the Investing Universe

THE TEN QUESTIONS

1. What is it?
2. **Is it investing, speculating, or gambling?**
3. What is the upside?
4. What is the downside?
5. Who is on the other side of the trade?
6. What is the investment vehicle?
7. What does it take to be successful?
8. Who is getting a cut?
9. How does it impact your portfolio?
10. Should you invest?

QUESTION TWO: IS IT INVESTING, SPECULATING, OR GAMBLING?

Classifying financial opportunities by whether they have a greater likelihood to be profitable, to be unprofitable, or to have an outcome that is highly uncertain simplifies the investing universe. Our research time is reduced when we focus most of our efforts on financial opportunities that have a positive expected return.

I visited the Grand Canyon for the first time several years ago. I have flown over it on numerous occasions, but I had never managed to drive there. My family and I stopped at the south rim of the canyon. It was cold, so we huddled into the Desert View Watchtower, which was designed by architect Mary Colter and completed in 1932. The main floor of the tower has several black mirrors trimmed with thick wood attached to the window frames. A placard on one of the mirrors describes them as reflectoscopes, but they are also known as Claude mirrors, after seventeenth-century painter Claude Lorrain.

Viewing the reflection of the Grand Canyon in a Claude mirror does several things. It frames a view so the magnificent scale of the Grand Canyon is reduced to a digestible whole. Framing is about setting limits. When artists choose a scene to paint or photographers a subject to photograph, they are framing. They limit their view to perhaps 10 degrees of their 120-degree peripheral vision. When we limit our material possessions, we are framing. When we prune the number of activities we pursue, we are framing. When we limit our investing to asset classes we can explain in simple terms, we are also framing.

Not only does a Claude mirror frame a scene, but the use of black glass adds a smokiness filter to the reflection that better allows the human eye to detect the differences among different colors and shades—to make comparisons.[1] Just as a Claude mirror helped artists simplify and frame a scene and made it easier to compare different colors and shades, using the ten-question framework detailed in this book will allow you to simplify the investing world and make it easier to compare different investment opportunities.

A question that can help us simplify and compare is to ask, "Is it investing, speculating, or gambling?" Answering this question segments the investing universe into three areas:

1. **INVESTMENTS.** Opportunities that have a greater likelihood of being profitable
2. **SPECULATION.** Opportunities where the investment outcome is highly uncertain
3. **GAMBLING.** Opportunities that have a greater likelihood of losing money

I first grasped the difference between investing, speculating, and gambling as a child, even if I didn't know what those words meant. Each year, the Catholic parish in Cincinnati where I attended elementary school held a fund-raising festival. My parents would give me $5 to buy tickets that I could then spend at the various booths and activities. My favorite booth was a game called Post Office. I'd give the attendant a ticket and then choose one of the ten windows that were fitted into a wooden case. Behind each glass pane there was a stack of wrapped prizes. That was it. Present a ticket; choose a window; get a prize. The excitement was in the uncertainty of not knowing what the prize would be, but in my five-year-old mind the prize was always worth more than what I paid. There was a positive payoff.

WHAT IS INVESTING?

Dr. Kingsley Jones, founder of the investment firm Jevons Global, in a paper on financial literacy described investing as "a bet of prospective *posi-*

tive return, with reasonable statistical reliability."[2] That describes my experience playing the Post Office game. It was a bet that statistically always paid off with a prize that for me was always worth more than my initial investment. Of course, given that this was a charity event, on average the prizes were probably worth less than what I paid, but I was playing with my parents' money. Hence, the game always had a positive payoff for me. A true investment will have a positive expected return not because the investor is playing with free money, but due to the attributes of the asset itself.

For example, stocks, bonds, and real estate can be classified as investments because they have positive expected returns. That expectation is statistically reliable because these investments usually generate income in the form of dividends, interest, or rent. If a stock doesn't pay a dividend, the underlying company usually has earnings that are reinvested back in the company, implying that someday the company will pay a dividend. That doesn't mean an investment will always have a positive return, but over the long term there is a reasonable expectation that it will.

WHAT IS SPECULATING?

The town in Ohio where I grew up also held an annual carnival, where a touring company set up Ferris wheels, slides, and game booths. Many of the games involved tossing, throwing, or shooting something to win a prize. I usually avoided these games because I hated to lose, but when I was about ten, one of the carnival booths had a ring toss where one of the prizes was a pair of handcuffs. I wanted those handcuffs.

The carnival was held over three days in the high school parking lot near my house, and for three days I debated whether I should risk my money in hopes of winning the handcuffs. I would walk by the booth and glance at the distance between the tossing area and the peg with the handcuffs attached and imagine throwing the ring and winning the prize. Finally, on the last day of the carnival, I took a few dollars from my piggy bank and went to the booth to try to win the handcuffs.

Dr. Kingsley Jones describes a speculation as a "bet about which there is viable disagreement on the sign of the return," or in other words, whether the financial instrument will rise or fall in price.[3] The ring toss game was not rigged. It was a simple game of skill. The carnival booth stayed in business because most of the players didn't have the skill to win. But for any given player, it was uncertain whether he or she would win or lose. Alas, in my case, I proved unskillful and unlucky. I lost my money and didn't win the handcuffs.

Uncertainty regarding the rate of return for a speculation exists because there usually isn't any income generated by the asset in the form of interest, dividends, or rent. The only way to make a profit with a speculation is to sell the asset to someone in the future who is willing to pay more than what you paid. The big unknown is whether investors in the future will be willing to pay more for the item. Examples of speculative assets include collectibles, such as art and antiques; commodities, such as gold and oil futures; currencies, including the U.S. dollar; and cryptocurrencies, such as Bitcoin.

Speculating in Comic Books, Tulips, and Bitcoin

I have a friend who has been debating whether to buy issue one of the Batman comic book series. It is grade two, so it is not in mint condition, but it still sells for upward of $50,000. Is this comic book overpriced? There is no way to tell. It is worth whatever speculators are willing to pay for it. Speculating in comic books is no different from speculating in tulips.

In the late sixteenth century, tulips were introduced to the Netherlands for the first time, as travelers brought them back from Turkey. Hobbyists began to trade and eventually sell tulip bulbs to each other. By the early seventeenth century, more and more individuals were attracted to the tulip trade, especially to rare and exotic bulbs.[4] In 1618, Dutch botanist Joost van Ravelingen wrote of tulips, "Here in this country people value most the flamed, winged, speckled, jagged, shredded, and the most variegated count for most, and the ones that are the most valued are not the most beautiful or the nicest, but the ones which are the rarest to find."[5]

Prices for tulip bulbs increased throughout the 1620s and 1630s. In the mid-1630s, a number of partnerships and companies were set up to trade tulip bulbs via auctions and private sales. Then in the summer of 1636, tulip bulb prices skyrocketed before crashing in February, 1637. Anne Goldgar, in her book on tulip mania, writes of the speculative frenzy: "After the fact—as happened in other financial crises in later centuries—it is easy to preach irrationality, but there was nothing intrinsically crazy . . . about buying a product it was clear one could sell at a higher price. The unsustainability of the price was not predictable, and if a crash happened, it was not necessarily to be foreseen."[6]

A modern-day version of tulip mania may be what is going on with the cryptocurrency Bitcoin. I own some as a speculation. I have studied Bitcoin at length, and I can explain what it is and how it works. My investment thesis is that Bitcoin will be more valuable because the supply is capped at 21 million coins; however, this only works if participants trust it and want to own it. If it falls out of favor and turns out to be just a fad, then I will lose money on this speculation.

In January 2018, Bitcoin experienced huge price swings as it fell from its high that month of over $17,000 per Bitcoin to a little over $10,000, a 40% decline. After one of those sharp sell-offs, I received an e-mail from a listener of my podcast asking what I thought about the Bitcoin dip. Later that day, a friend texted me asking whether he should buy more Bitcoin. Speculation means there is extreme uncertainty about whether the asset will rise or fall in price. A 40% decline is not a dip. A dip suggests a temporary setback before the price continues to climb, but with a speculative asset there is no way to know if it will rebound or continue to plummet. There isn't a correct price because there is no income to determine if the price is too high or too low.

Investments differ from speculations because there are objective measures to determine if the asset is valued more or less than its historical average. For example, with a stock you can observe the price that investors are willing to pay for a dollar's worth of earnings, which is known as the price-to-earnings ratio. An investor can compare a stock's current P/E ratio with its historical P/E ratio and with the P/E ratio of companies in the same industry. This allows the investor to make a judgment about whether the stock has a lower or higher valuation relative to its historical average or to its peers.

With a speculation, historical comparisons are difficult because there aren't earnings or income streams to compare the price against to determine if the asset is cheap or expensive. All we have are the historical prices and perhaps some data on supply and demand for certain speculative assets like commodities.

Speculating in Oil

I know a number of professional commodities traders who work for big institutional trading firms. Commodities are hard assets such as agricultural products (e.g., wheat, corn), metals (e.g., copper, gold), and energy sources (e.g., oil, natural gas). These commodity traders work in an extremely competitive field as they compete with other traders and with computer algorithms to make a profit. One oil trader mentioned to me that "no one can trade oil without customer flow." What he meant was that unless an oil trader is able to see data on how much oil is being produced, refined, consumed, and stored, and what the order flow data is for speculators and hedgers buying oil futures, then it will be extremely difficult to make money trading oil. Even professional traders with that knowledge now find it difficult to make a profit in oil futures as they compete more and more with computer algorithms.

The U.S. Commodity Futures Trading Commission describes a commodity futures contract as an "agreement to buy or sell a particular commodity at a future date."[7] Many participants in the futures market are commodity producers such as farmers and miners seeking to protect against financial losses due to large price swings in underlying commodities. Other participants in the commodities futures market are speculators seeking to make a profit from price changes. These speculators include individual investors who sometimes buy crude oil investment vehicles simply because they believe the price of oil will rise. They often don't have a basis for this belief. It is just a feeling they have perhaps because oil went down in price, and they expect it to rebound. They "buy the dip."

Oil is an example of why we need to be able to describe what an investment is. As individual investors, we can't easily speculate on oil by buying and storing a barrel of crude oil in our basement in the same way we can speculate on gold when we buy gold coins. Investment vehicles, such as exchange-traded funds, can't easily buy and sell barrels of oil either. Instead, they buy and sell oil futures contracts.

When investors buy oil futures contracts, they are promising to take delivery of oil on a specific day in the future. In practice, investors usually exit these contracts before they expire, so they don't actually take delivery; or some oil futures contracts are settled in cash. The price of oil delivered in the future usually differs from today's price, which is known as the spot price. The spot price might be $60 for a barrel of light crude oil delivered today to Cushing, Oklahoma. Meanwhile, today's price for a futures contract for a barrel of light crude oil to be delivered 30 days from now might be $64. If investors buy that futures contract today, they will only make a profit if 30 days from now the spot price of oil is above $64. If it rises to $63, although that is greater than today's price, they will still lose money.

Investors in futures contracts benefit when the spot price at maturity turns out to be higher than expected when they entered into the contract. Investors lose when the spot price is lower than anticipated. In other words, investors only make money investing in oil futures if the price when the contract expires is higher than what investors expected it to be when the contract was created. Therefore, when investors speculate on oil, they aren't just speculating that the price will increase. They are also speculating that the price of oil will go up by more than what other speculators expect it to be in the future.

Sound confusing? It is. But oil futures nicely illustrate why we need to understand an investment in order to successfully invest in it. Having a feeling something will go up in price is a lousy basis for making long-term investment decisions. Unfortunately, speculations are often made based on feelings. I know because I have made them.

ATTEMPTING TO DAY-TRADE

As an investment advisor, I once visited a commodities hedge fund located in a Connecticut mansion. The trading floor was divided. Math whizzes, who were building, testing, and implementing algorithms to trade commodities, sat on one side of the room at neat and orderly desks. On the other half of the trading floor, the discretionary traders sat. They made trades based on their knowledge and instinct. They seemed more laid-back. Their desks were messier, and a number of traders had guitars and other stress relievers sitting on or beside their desks. They were brilliant traders, which is why they worked for a hedge fund. Seeing them in person made me think that I could be a trader if I worked at it.

A couple of years later, after I quit the investment business, I tried my hand at trading. I opened an account and traded oil futures, precious metals, interest rate futures, and currencies. I had no customer flow information. I had only feelings based on price trends and economic data. A few trades were profitable, but most lost money. I also found the volatility from hour to hour and day to day to be unsettling. After six months, I ended my experiment, but not before losing $20,000 on one trade because I forgot to close out an open position in silver, which fell in price before I realized my mistake and was able to exit the trade.

In my short-lived career as a trader, I found I had no competitive edge to ensure a consistent profit. I was guessing, which is often what speculating entails. Buying something, hoping it will go up in price. Of course, I knew this was an experiment going into it, so I had only risked a small amount of my net worth. Unfortunately, I have known individuals who, due to their overconfidence in their forecasting abilities, risked much more speculating in commodities and learned the same lessons I did. Only they suffered horrendous financial losses as a result. There is nothing wrong with speculating, but given there is no way to determine the right price for a speculative asset since there is no income, you should allocate less than 10% of your investment portfolio to speculations. The vast majority of your portfolio and your research time should be focused on investments that have a positive expected return. Consequently, most of this book covers investing, not speculation.

WHAT IS GAMBLING?

There was another game at my parish festival that I only played once. It was called Big Six. It was a game of chance that involved placing a bet on a specific number. After the players made a bet, the attendant would spin a wooden wheel with metal pins that hit a rubber pointer, creating a loud clicking sound that filled the festival hall. Eventually the wheel would stop, and if the pointer rested on your chosen number, you won. I don't remember how many numbers were on the wheel. I just remember the clicking sound and the sickening disappointment I felt when I didn't win.

The UNLV Center for Gaming Research measured the results for a single Big Six table game at an Atlantic City casino from January 2007 to December 2010. This game offered payouts as high as 45 to 1, which means a player could potentially win $45 for a $1 bet. The average monthly winning percentage for Big Six players during the four-year measurement period was 42.25%. The players lost close to 60% of the time, which led the UNLV Center for Gaming Research to conclude that Big Six "was one of the worst bets on the casino floor for gamblers," and "it is a game to be avoided."[8]

Dr. Kingsley Jones describes a gamble as "a bet of prospective *negative return*, with reasonable statistical reliability." If you gamble over a long enough period of time, you will more than likely suffer losses and eventually lose all your investment. Jones writes, "Customers who cannot reasonably expect a positive return from a financial product should properly be sold on the entertainment to be had from losing their money."[9]

Binary Options

Binary options are an example of a financial product that can be akin to gambling, depending on how the contracts are structured. A binary option is a security where an investor pays a premium and places a bet on whether the underlying asset that the option contract is based on will increase or decrease in value. If the option expires just one tick in the investor's favor in that it closes above or below the target price, the investor is paid $100 per contract. If it doesn't, the investor loses the entire premium paid. The time frame for binary options can be a few minutes, hours, a day, or weeks.[10] Nadex, a binary options exchange, says of these options, "You only have to be a little bit right to get the maximum profit."[11] It doesn't mention that you only have to be a little bit wrong to suffer the maximum loss.

Nadex serves as an exchange, so for every winning trade, there is a loser on the other side. Consequently, trading binary options on an exchange is more like a speculation. Yet some binary option marketplaces are not exchanges. The traders interact directly with the options sponsor that structures the contracts, has capital at stake, and pays out winnings from its own resources. This is clearly a gambling situation, because if the trader's expected return was positive, then the options provider would have a negative expected return. The options sponsor would eventually go bust, just like a casino would go broke if slot machines paid out more than they take in. Knowing whom we are trading with and how the financial opportunity is structured is key to determining if it is investing, speculating, or gambling.

Our analysis of investing, speculating, and gambling has focused on the characteristics of the underlying asset, but as individuals we also play a role in whether an asset in our portfolio is an investment or a gamble. If we don't do the work to understand an investment, an asset that might have a positive expected return for most investors might actually have a negative expected return for us, meaning it would be closer to gambling than investing. The investment discipline of answering specific questions about an investment opportunity will help ensure we aren't gambling due to our lack of knowledge.

CHAPTER SUMMARY

- Just as a Claude mirror helped artists simplify and frame a scene, this book's ten-question framework helps you simplify the investing world and makes it easier to compare different investment opportunities.

- Investments are assets with positive expected returns, usually because there is a cash flow component. Examples of investments include stocks, bonds, and real estate.

- Speculations are assets where the outcome is highly uncertain and there is viable disagreement about whether they will rise or fall in price. Examples of speculations include collectibles, such as art and antiques; commodities, such as gold and oil futures; currencies, including the dollar; and cryptocurrencies, such as Bitcoin.

- Investments differ from speculations in that investments usually generate income and have objective measures such as the price-to-earnings ratio to determine if the asset is valued more or less than its historical average.

- We should allocate less than 10% of our portfolio to speculations. The other 90%, or more, of our portfolio and research time should be focused on investments that have a positive expected payoff.

- Gambles are bets with expected negative returns and should be undertaken only to be entertained.

3

What Is the Upside?

Rules of Thumb for Estimating Investment Returns

THE TEN QUESTIONS

1. What is it?
2. Is it investing, speculating, or gambling?
3. **What is the upside?**
4. What is the downside?
5. Who is on the other side of the trade?
6. What is the investment vehicle?
7. What does it take to be successful?
8. Who is getting a cut?
9. How does it impact your portfolio?
10. Should you invest?

QUESTION THREE: WHAT IS THE UPSIDE?

We can use rules of thumb to estimate an investment's expected return. This allows us to compare different opportunities and make sure our assumptions are reasonable.

A listener to my podcast has a financial predicament. It is a good predicament, but one he finds to be emotionally exhausting. He works for a start-up company that completed an initial public offering of stock. That means the company sold shares to the investing public for the first time to raise money for its founders, backers, and ongoing operations.

This listener received $1.5 million from this offering, a significant windfall. He wrote: "I am not sure how to wrap my head around this. I come from a lower middle class family, and I think at this point I could be described as wealthy, but with the more I have, the more I worry."[1] He decided to seek the help of a financial planner. The listener wrote: "Basically they ran a bunch of different scenarios of future income, housing, and so on, and the main conclusion that I get out of it is if we can keep our expenses around where they are today, we are very likely to be able to be financially independent before retirement age, and still leave a significant legacy behind. I think that all in all things seem well."

A FLAWED FINANCIAL PLAN

The listener sent me the financial plan. It is 79 pages long and compares his current situation with five different financial scenarios with plenty of charts and graphs. It paints a favorable financial picture for him, his wife, and their two children. He concluded based on the plan that he could retire right then at age 41 with a net worth of $1.8 million and never run out of money if he achieved the plan's 7.6% expected portfolio return.

That return estimate made me pause. A 7.6% expected annualized return seemed high. I dug through the financial plan and found the asset class return assumptions on page 70. The plan assumed that the future returns for stocks and bonds would be the same as they had been in the past. In the early years of my investment career, I also used historical returns as the basis for what I expected in the future. Then I got burned and realized how dangerous it is to naively assume that historical returns will be repeated in the future. Here is how I learned that lesson.

Earlier I shared how one of my first clients told me that if he couldn't explain a new investment opportunity to another board member who wasn't on the committee in a way that the member could understand, then the university shouldn't invest. Each quarter, I met with this investment committee on the fifty-fourth floor of an Indianapolis skyscraper with an incredible view of the cityscape and cornfields that stretched for miles in all directions. I felt as if I were on top of the world as I looked out that boardroom window. At other times, I thought: "What in the world am I doing here? Who am I to be advising this committee on how to allocate its alma mater's investment portfolio?" My transportation to and from the meetings was a white Toyota Tercel with huge black bumpers. The car had a four-speed manual transmission, and it smelled like plastic. It even came with an extra four-pack of plastic hubcaps in case the originals fell off. I parked that car several blocks from my meeting place so none of the committee members could see that their investment advisor couldn't afford a nicer car.

At the committee meeting in January 1998, I introduced the members to a new asset type that the university had not invested in previously. The asset category was non-investment-grade bonds, also known as high-yield bonds or junk bonds. Bonds are debt instruments issued by governments and corporations to raise money for new projects or ongoing operations. These entities pay investors interest on the debt and return the principal when the bond matures. Bonds differ from bank certificates of deposit (CDs) in that bonds can be sold more easily than CDs prior to maturity. Also, unlike CDs, bonds can fluctuate in price as interest rates change.

The committee members were familiar with bond investing through their existing bond manager, but high-yield bonds were new to them.

High-yield bonds are issued by riskier companies that have a lot of debt and have less of a buffer in terms of excess cash flow after making interest payments. Most bonds are rated by bond rating agencies based on the likelihood of issuer default, that is, failing to pay an interest or principal payment. Investment-grade bonds are the safest and have a very low risk of default. Non-investment-grade bonds (i.e., high-yield bonds) have a higher risk of default, but they also pay higher interest rates so they generate more income for investors as long as the high-yield bond issuer doesn't default.

I was a novice on non-investment-grade bonds, and most of my education on the sector came from high-yield bond managers who were more than happy to bring me up to speed on the bright prospects for this asset type while also emphasizing their expertise in selecting specific bonds. I apparently did a good enough job educating the committee members on high-yield bonds, passing the chair's "Can I explain it to someone else?" test. The committee members decided to allocate 5% of the portfolio to the asset category. At the next quarterly meeting, the committee selected a high-yield bond manager to oversee the allocation.

Back in my office, I was feeling good about my ability to advise this client when Fred, the founder of the advisory firm where I worked, asked me how things were going with this client. I proudly told him how the university had just invested in high-yield bonds.

"Why in the world would you recommend that?" he asked.

Taken aback by his critical tone, I replied with the default reason any good advisor uses to justify an investment decision: "Diversification." If an investment portfolio were a pot of soup, then diversifying means adding additional ingredients in order to make the soup taste better. Better, in the case of a portfolio, means the new addition will either increase the portfolio's expected return or lower its expected volatility. We'll explore diversification more in Chapter 9, but for now just know I thought that adding some high-yield bond spice to the university's investment soup was a smart and tasty move.

Fred ticked off a number of reasons why it was a terrible time to invest in high-yield bonds. There was too much investor money flooding into the sector, pushing down yields and lowering expected returns. There were also too many bonds being issued by companies to build out telecommunications infrastructure for the expanding internet, which could lead to overcapacity and to higher bond defaults in the future, also reducing returns. All of Fred's reasons were forward looking, while all my justifications for recommending high-yield bonds to this client were backward looking. High-yield bonds had performed incredibly well over the previous five years, and I expected them to continue to do so.

It turned out Fred was right. The high-yield bond manager did fine for a year or so, but when it became clear that there was too much telecommunications capacity, default rates for high-yield bonds rose. The allocation severely underperformed the university's more conservative bond manager. Each quarter for several years after making that ill-timed high-yield bond allocation, I had to sit and explain to the committee members why high-yield bonds were doing so poorly. I felt awful and never forgot that feeling of recommending such a poorly performing asset class. While the investment didn't lose money, it did lower the university's overall return, and lagged the existing more conservative bond manager.

A Classic Investment Mistake

My mistake with this client was I became enamored with the historical performance of high-yield bonds. I neglected to look at the primary drivers of those historical returns and the starting conditions at the time we invested to see what would have to happen for the historical returns to be repeated in the future.

At this point, you may be saying to yourself, "I don't have the time or the skill to be researching bonds or stocks to know what returns will be in the future." It turns out, it is not as difficult as you think. We don't need to know everything about every single investment. We just need to know enough to make effective decisions. Let me explain.

A couple of years ago, my wife, LaPriel, and I spent part of the winter in southern Mexico, where we rented a car for a month. This rental reminded me of my gutless Toyota Tercel that I drove to my investment meetings and kept hidden from my clients. The rental car was a Volkswagen Gol, a Brazilian-made vehicle with a 1.6-liter engine and 101 horsepower. It had a four-speed manual transmission and cost $9,200 new. I know this, because in negotiating the rental contract, $9,200 is the amount the Budget Rental Car office in Playa del Carmen took as a deposit on my American Express card after I declined the "optional" insurance coverage since I was covered through my card.

Several weeks into our trip, we were in the city of Campeche at the bottom of a hill on a street that must rank among the steepest in North America. I hesitated for a moment, but then decided to go for it. About halfway up the hill, the RPMs were high enough to shift into second gear. I did so, and that was a mistake—five seconds later the gradient got steeper, and the car could no longer climb with the transmission in second. The VW stopped before I could get it back into first gear. There we sat: my feet on the brake and clutch, our backs pressed against the seats, looking toward the sky. The first thing that came to my mind was a video taken in Moab, Utah, of an out-of-control Jeep careening backward down a steep incline and then crashing. The second thing I considered was the $9,200 deposit on the car.

Harvard physicist Lisa Randall wrote: "We all work in terms of effective theories. We find descriptions that match what we actually see, interact with, and measure. The fact that a more fundamental description can underlie what we observe is pretty much irrelevant until we have access to any effects that differentiate that description."[2] She points out how Newton's laws work well for constructing a bridge that won't collapse or sending a satellite to space. Or in my case to describe what would happen when I released the brake on the VW Gol while resting on a hill if I were unable to engage the clutch fast enough. Yet Randall points out that "Newton's laws are approximations that work at relatively low speeds and for large macroscopic objects."[3] Quantum mechanics and the theory of relativity are deeper theories that underlie Newton's laws. I didn't need to know quantum mechanics to escape from my hill predicament. I needed to know about gravity. I did a quick analysis and determined that my embarrassment from easing the car backward down the hill was a price I was willing to pay to avoid the potential financial cost and personal injury from crashing if I tried to go forward and couldn't put the car into gear in time.

Effective theory is how we approach all areas of our lives. There is too much information to know every detail about every topic. Randall writes: "We use a map that has the scale we need. It's pointless to know all the small streets around you when you're barreling down a highway."[4] One way we do this is by using rules of thumb.

RULES OF THUMB

Rules of thumb are simple patterns we can follow that are derived from underlying principles. They are shortcuts for applying effective theories to solve specific problems. For example, if you travel a lot, you soon realize one of the small challenges with staying in different places is figuring out how the shower works. It is amazing how many different types of faucet mechanisms there are.

The three rules of thumb for operating a shower are:

1. Turn the water on.
2. Adjust the water temperature.
3. Engage the mechanism to run a shower instead of a bath.

You don't need to be a plumbing expert with an intricate knowledge of the inner workings of a faucet to run a shower. You just need to apply the rules of thumb. Each shower you encounter might be slightly different, but the underlying principles of an effective shower remain constant: Turn the water on, adjust the water temperature, and direct the water to the shower head.

Likewise, there are underlying principles that determine the long-term return for asset classes such as stocks, bonds, and rental real estate that we can use to develop rules of thumb for estimating future returns. The three drivers of asset class performance are:

1. **CASH FLOW.** The income from interest, dividends, or rents that is distributed to the asset owner. For estimating returns, the income is expressed as a percentage of the asset's market value such as a dividend yield or a bond yield.
2. **CASH FLOW GROWTH.** How the income stream or cash flow grows over time. This is usually expressed as an annual percentage growth rate of dividends or earnings on a per share basis.
3. **CHANGE IN VALUATION.** What investors are willing to pay for the income stream now versus later. This repricing is usually expressed as the annual percentage change in an asset due to a change in a valuation measure related to the income or earnings such as the price-to-earnings ratio or price-to-dividend ratio for stocks.[5]

The first two drivers that compose these rules of thumb reflect the math of investing with regard to how cash flow is generated and grows. In the case of bonds, their returns are primarily driven by prevailing interest rates at the time the investment is undertaken. For most bonds, the interest payments received stay the same from one period to the next, so there is no cash flow growth. The exception would be variable-rate bonds, where the interest cash flow can vary from one period to the next as interest rates change. The third driver reflects the emotion of investing in terms of how much investors are willing to pay for that cash flow. The measure of emotion for corporate bond investing is reflected in fluctuations in the additional interest rate yield or spread that investors demand above the yield on relatively risk-free U.S. Treasury bonds to compensate investors for potential default risk.

In the midst of the U.S. recession in 1990, investors demanded a large premium to protect against high-yield bond defaults.[6] Investors were fearful, and so high-yield bonds yielded 12% more than the ten-year U.S. Treasury bonds. Eight years later when I recommended the non-investment-grade bond allocation to my university client, the spread between high-yield bonds and ten-year U.S. Treasury bonds had fallen to less than 3%. This narrowing spread was driven by large inflows into high-yield bond mutual funds from zealous investors chasing after the strong returns the sector had experienced. By December 2000, almost three years after the university made its investment, non-investment-grade bond yield spreads were back to 9%, which means the value of the bonds fell as their yields rose and defaults increased.

I should have been more aware of the emotion of bond investing when I made the recommendation to invest. It would have been better to invest in high-yield bonds when spreads were wide and investors were fearful, such as in 2000 when the high-yield bond spread was 9% rather than 3% when we initiated the investment. Even if defaults increased during a recession, getting the higher yield above U.S. Treasury bonds would have more than compensated for the defaults.

I had a much better understanding of the math and emotion of bond investing by the time the global financial crisis hit in 2008. In early 2009, high-yield bonds were yielding 17% more than ten-year Treasury bonds. In that environment, once it became clear that the entire financial system wasn't going to collapse, we increased our clients' allocation to high-yield bonds, and I also increased the allocation in my personal portfolio. This time my clients did extremely well, earning double-digit returns on their bond investments.

ESTIMATING BOND RETURNS

The following section on bonds might seem a bit challenging. You may want to read it over a couple of times. Once you understand these bond basics, an entire asset class will appear much less threatening, as you will have an effective theory—rules of thumb—for bond investing.

To estimate the return of an individual bond or a bond mutual fund or bond ETF, the primary piece of information you need is the bond's or fund's yield to maturity. This is an estimate of the annualized return for a bond or for the bonds held within a fund if they are held until maturity. Maturity is the term used to describe when a bond returns its principal outstanding and stops paying interest. Sometimes bonds can be redeemed early. This is known as a bond being called. There is an additional calculation called yield to worst, which is an estimate of a bond or bond fund's return if the bonds are held to maturity or until they are called, depending on which is more likely. I am not sure why it is called yield to worst other than perhaps bond investors don't like to have their bond holdings called early because then they have to find a different bond to invest in.

In the United States, each bond mutual fund or ETF is required to publish its SEC yield, which is effectively the fund's yield to worst minus its operating expenses, such as the investment management fee charged by the mutual fund or ETF. For example, suppose the SEC yield for the Vanguard Total Bond Market Index Fund is 3.0%. If investors hold this bond fund for at least seven years, their return will be close to 3.0% annualized. If they hold it for shorter periods, the return could be less or greater than that, depending on whether interest rates rise or fall. That is how bond math works. I explain where the minimum seven-year holding period comes from later in this chapter.

There are, of course, thick books, such as the 1,840-page *Handbook of Fixed Income Securities* edited by Frank J. Fabozzi, that go into excruciating detail on bond math and fixed-income investing, but as individual investors we don't need to be bond experts. We don't need to know the quantum mechanics of bonds. We just need to know the basics of bond gravity—the rules of thumb that allow us to effectively invest. And the fundamental rule of thumb for investing in bond funds and ETFs is that the best estimate of their future return for holding periods of seven years or more is their current SEC yield, yield to maturity, or yield to worst. These yield metrics represent the cash flow component distributed to the asset owner as expressed in the rules of thumb for estimating asset class returns that I shared earlier.

In my listener's financial plan, the yield to maturity for U.S. bonds at the time the planner completed his analysis in August 2017 was 2.2%. Yet he assumed bonds would return 4.8% annualized in the plan because that is what bonds had returned over the previous 15 years. With a starting yield of 2.2%, it is mathematically impossible for bonds to return 4.8% annualized over a holding period longer than seven years.

The 15-year historical period the planner used for his bond return estimate went from September 30, 2001, through September 30, 2016. What were 10-year U.S. Treasury bonds yielding in September 2001? 4.6%. In other words, the historical bond return of 4.8% annualized used in the financial plan came in very close to the starting yield just as we would expect. It wasn't exact because the bond index the planner used included some corporate bonds, which, as we have seen, will yield more than U.S. government bonds to compensate investors for the potential default risk.

Bonds and Interest Rates

One of the few things I remember from my introductory finance class in university was Professor Barngrover standing in front of class rhythmically clapping as he repeated over and over again, "As interest rates go up, the value of bonds goes down." Likewise, he repeated the mantra, "As interest rates go down, the value of bonds goes up."[7]

Why do bond prices fall when interest rates increase and rise when interest rates decline? Consider an investor who bought a newly issued

30-year U.S. Treasury bond that yields 3%. The bond pays $30 in interest annually for every $1,000 of bond face value. The face value is the price of the bond that the interest payments are based on. If interest rates rise to 4%, then an investor who buys a newly issued 30-year bond would receive $40 in annual interest.

Seeing that an investor can now buy a new bond that pays $40 in interest while the old bond pays only $30, the old bond's price must fall to a level that an investor would be economically indifferent to investing in either of the two bonds. In other words, the price of the old bond must fall to a level at which investors will make the same amount of money holding the old bond as they would owning the new bond.

Bond Duration

The degree to which a bond's price changes as interest rates fluctuate depends on when the bond matures, its yield, and other features. A bond's or bond portfolio's price sensitivity to changing interest rates is known as its duration. Duration is calculated by taking the weighted average maturity of a bond's or bond portfolio's cash flows in terms of the interest and principal payments. Bonds have maturities of less than 1 month to over 30 years. The longer a bond's or bond fund's maturity, the higher its duration will be. A 30-year bond receives cash payments in the form of interest for three decades compared with just a few years for a 5-year bond. Consequently, the duration or weighted average maturity of the cash flows for a 30-year bond will be much higher than for a 5-year bond. The higher (i.e., longer) a bond's or bond fund's duration, the more its price will change as interest rates change. More specifically, a 1% increase or decrease in interest rates will cause an individual bond or bond fund/ETF to fall or rise in price by roughly the amount of its duration. For example, suppose you have two bond funds, one with a 6-year duration and one with a 2-year duration. If there were a 1% increase in interest rates, the bond fund with a 6-year duration would fall in price by approximately 6%, and the bond fund with a 2-year duration would fall in price by approximately 2%.

Earlier I wrote that we could use a bond fund's SEC yield to estimate its annualized return for a seven-year or greater holding period. That isn't true, however, for shorter holding periods. Over shorter-term periods, the fund's duration will influence its return because its price could rise or fall as interest rates change. But over longer holding periods, if interest rates rise, the price decline the bond fund experiences gets offset by the higher interest payments the bond fund receives as it reinvests interest and principal payments in higher-yielding bonds. Consequently, investors can look at today's SEC yield for a fund or ETF and feel quite confident that it is a reasonable estimate for the fund's annualized return if they hold it for seven years or more. That will allow sufficient time for interest income received by the fund to offset any price fluctuations due to changing interest rates.

Bond Defaults

There is one caveat with this bond expected return analysis. It assumes there aren't any bonds held by the fund or ETF that default. For most bond funds, that is a reasonable assumption if the funds hold mostly government bonds, bonds backed by home mortgages, and investment-grade corporate bonds. But if the fund invests in non-investment-grade bonds, then we need to reduce the SEC yield by an estimate of the annual losses due to default.

The long-term average annual default rate for high-yield bonds in the United States has been approximately 4.2%.[8] When a bond defaults, investors don't typically lose all their money. Usually, there is some recovery as the bondholders negotiate with the entity that defaulted. The average recovery for defaulted high-yield bonds has been about 39%.[9] That equates to a loss of 61%. Therefore, a reasonable assumption for high-yield bonds is to reduce the estimated annualized return derived from the

SEC yield by 2.6%. This represents the 4.2% annual default after adjusting for recoveries (i.e., 4.2% default times 61% loss = 2.6%).

For example, suppose the SEC yield for the SPDR Bloomberg Barclays High Yield Bond ETF is 6.0%. Meanwhile, let's assume the yield on ten-year Treasury bonds is 3.0%. We can calculate the high-yield bond spread by subtracting the 3.0% ten-year Treasury yield from the 6.0% SEC yield on the bond ETF. That works out to a spread of 3.0% before considering defaults. If we reduce that 6.0% SEC yield by 2.6% to reflect potential defaults, we would calculate a high-yield bond expected return for a seven- to ten-year holding period of 3.4% annualized. That's not very high compared with the 3.0% ten-year Treasury bond yield. That suggests in this scenario that investors are overly confident about the prospects for high-yield bonds, as the investors are not demanding a very high incremental yield premium or spread to hold them (i.e., only 3%). The long-term average incremental yield or spread for high-yield bonds compared with ten-year U.S. Treasury bonds is 5%.[10] When spreads are less than that, investors are overly zealous about non-investment-grade bonds, and returns will be lower. When spreads are greater than 5%—such as the 15% or more spread available to investors in 2009 at the end of the global financial crisis—investors are fearful, and future returns will likely be higher than average, even after taking into account higher defaults.

What Determines Interest Rates

We have seen that the best estimate of a bond fund's return for holding periods of seven years or more is the current SEC yield, yield to maturity, or yield to worst. In the case of high-yield bonds, the SEC yield should be reduced by at least 2.6% to account for potential defaults. That is the basic math of bond investing.

But why are interest rates high during some periods and low during others? In the mid- to late 1970s, my then single mother became a real estate agent at a time when 30-year mortgage rates in the United States were over 9%. By 1981 when she ended her unsuccessful real estate career, 30-year mortgage rates had peaked at over 18%. And 31 years later in 2012, 30-year mortgage rates bottomed at 3.3%.

How could 30-year mortgages and other interest rates be over 18% in 1981 and close to 3% in 2012? It comes back to math and emotion. Prevailing interest rates are based on investors' expectations and how much additional compensation investors demand for uncertainty regarding those expectations. The nominal yield on a bond, say a ten-year U.S. Treasury bond, can be broken down into investors' expectations regarding inflation and what is known as the real, or after-inflation, yield. Inflation measures the rise in prices over time. If investors believe inflation will be high, then interest rates will also be high. In 1981, investors expected extremely high inflation.

We can observe investors' inflation expectations by comparing the yield on government bonds with the yield on inflation-protected government bonds, which in the United States are known as Treasury Inflation-Protected Securities, or TIPS. For example, if the yield on ten-year U.S. Treasury bonds is 3% and the yield on ten-year TIPS is 1%, then the market's inflation expectation is 2%, the difference between the nominal ten-year yield and the TIPS yield. The TIPS yield is also known as the real yield.

What determines the real bond yield? Again, it is based on investors' expectations. Specifically, their expectation for what real interest rates will be in the future and an additional term premium. The term premium represents the additional yield that investors demand for uncertainty regarding whether inflation or real rates will be higher than expected. When investors are fearful about the path of future interest rates or higher-than-expected inflation, then the term premium will be high. During the period of high inflation and high uncertainty in the United States in the early 1980s, the term premium was over 3% and contributed to yields on ten-year Treasury bonds well in excess of 10%.

At other times, during calmer periods when investors are confident in the future path of interest rates and the level of inflation, they require a small term premium, as they did in 2012 when interest rates were extremely low.

Comparing Bond Opportunities

In comparing various bond investment opportunities, you need to know:

1. The SEC yield, yield to maturity, or yield to worst
2. The duration
3. The average credit quality

You can find the SEC yield, yield to maturity, or yield to worst on the fund's or ETF's website, on Morningstar.com, or for individual bonds on your broker's website. These bond yield metrics are the best estimate of the opportunity's expected return over a seven- to ten-year holding period. The duration measures how sensitive the opportunity will be to fluctuating interest rates in the short-to-intermediate term. The greater the duration, the greater the price decline if interest rates rise. The average credit quality gives you a sense of how much of the yield is due to higher-risk non-investment-grade bonds. Funds or bonds rated AAA, AA, A, or BBB are considered investment grade and have a low risk of default. Funds or bonds rated BB, B, or C are non-investment grade and have a higher risk of default. Note that these are bond ratings by S&P. Other providers, such as Moody's, have similar categories, but their letter designations will be slightly different.

Since longer- (i.e., higher-) duration bond offerings typically have higher yields, as an investor you need to decide whether the additional yield is worth the potential volatility of a more interest rate–sensitive bond vehicle. For example, you might evaluate the difference between investing in an ultra-short-term bond fund with an SEC yield of 2.0%

and a duration of 0.6 year and investing in an intermediate-term bond fund with an SEC yield of 3.5% and a duration of 6 years. Is the additional 1.5% yield worth the additional volatility of a fund whose duration is ten times higher than a shorter-term bond fund? Probably not, unless you believe interest rates will fall, allowing for greater price appreciation for the longer-term bond fund. (See Table 3.1.)

TABLE 3.1   Bond Example

Bond Type	SEC Yield	Duration	Rate of Return After Estimated Defaults	Growth Above 2% Inflation
Ultra-short-term bond ETF	2.0%	0.6 year	—	0%
Intermediate-term bond ETF	3.5%	6.0 years	—	1.5%
High-yield bond ETF	6.0%	4.0 years	3.4%	1.4%

At the same time, at those low nominal yields, both funds barely keep up with let's say a 2% expected inflation rate, which is the inflation expectation derived from subtracting the yield on TIPS from the yield on regular government bonds. The low yields mean investors are quite confident that future interest rates will remain low and inflation won't be higher than 2%, as evidenced by their willingness to accept a very low term premium to protect against those risks.

Given those low yields, perhaps you decide to evaluate a high-yield bond fund or ETF as an alternative. Again, you look at the fund's SEC yield, which we will assume is 6.0% in our example, and reduce it by 2.6% to adjust for potential defaults, bringing its expected seven- to ten-year return to 3.4%. The fund has a four-year duration. Is it worth it? Probably not, if we assume that ten-year Treasury bond yields are 3%. That means the incremental yield or spread for high-yield bonds relative to ten-year Treasury bond yields (before taking into account potential defaults) is only 3.0% compared with the historical 5% average spread.

Financial Plan Revisited

My listener's financial planner assumed a 29% allocation to bonds, so if we lower the expected return for bonds to 2.2% (the bond yield at the time he produced the plan) from 4.8%, the overall expected portfolio return is reduced to 6.9% from 7.6%. That is a slightly more reasonable return expectation, but it is still flawed because the planner also used historical returns to estimate the future returns for stocks. The average stock return assumption he used in the plan was 9.8%. Is a close to 10% return for stocks a reasonable assumption? To answer that we need to apply the rules of thumb of cash flow, cash flow growth, and change in cash flow multiple to determine the upside or expected return for stocks.

ESTIMATING STOCK RETURNS

Let's look at how the three return drivers that constitute our rules of thumb influenced the historical returns for stocks. From January 1871 through July 2017, U.S. stocks returned 8.9% annualized. That 8.9% return can be divided into the three components, or performance drivers. The largest component, 4.5%, came from the dividend yield, which represents the cash flow or share of profits paid to shareholders over time. That's the first return driver.

The next largest component, 3.6%, came from growth in dividends per share, which reflects how the income stream or dividends grew over time. That's the second return driver of cash flow growth. A company can only increase its dividend payments if its earnings are growing.

The smallest component, 0.8%, came from an increase in the price-to-earnings ratio, which represents how much investors were willing to pay for a dollar's worth of earnings. That is the third return driver representing a change in valuation. Since dividends are paid out of earnings, an increase in the P/E ratio for stocks also means investors are willing to pay more for the dividend income stream.

In 1871, the P/E ratio for U.S. stocks was 10, meaning investors were willing to pay $10 for every dollar of earnings. By July 2017, the P/E ratio for stocks was 23. Investors were paying more for earnings, which means the valuation for stocks increased. If investors had only been willing to pay as much in 2017 for earnings as they did in 1871, the annualized return for U.S. stocks from 1871 to 2017 would have been approximately 8% instead of 8.9%, the sum of the dividend and earnings component.[11]

The dividends and earnings growth represent the math of stock investing, while the change in valuation reflects the emotion. At times, investors are optimistic and are willing to pay more for stocks. At other times, they are pessimistic and fearful and are willing to pay less. Separating the historical performance of stocks into three return drivers is an approximation, but there is a close enough relationship to explain the bulk of historical performance. Consequently, we can use those same return drivers to estimate the future returns for stocks.

A Closer Look at One Stock

To grasp the math behind this concept, let's examine one stock. You might need to read over this example a few times to understand it. You can also refer to Tables 3.2 and 3.3.

Let's assume a stock is selling for $40.00 per share and has earnings of $4.00. The price-to-earnings ratio is 10x, which is the $40.00 price divided by the $4.00 of earnings. Let's also assume the company pays out 25% of its earnings in dividends, so its starting annual dividend is $1.00 (i.e., 25% times $4.00 of earnings = $1.00 dividend). The 25% payout is known as the dividend payout ratio. Finally, the dividend yield is the dividend paid divided by the stock price, so our starting dividend yield is 2.5% (i.e., $1.00 dividend divided by the $40.00 price = 2.5% dividend yield).

If we assume that earnings grow 10% per year and that the price-to-earnings ratio stays at 10x, a reasonable estimate for the future return for the stock is the sum of the first two return drivers: the 2.5% dividend yield plus the 10% earnings per share growth for a return of 12.5% per year.

If the earnings actually grow at 10% per year, after three years the stock earnings per share would have grown from $4.00 to $5.32. If the price-to-earnings ratio is still 10x, then the stock price would have appreciated to $53.25 (i.e., 10 times $5.32 of earnings). Each year, the company pays 25% of the earnings as dividends, which means dividends also increase 10% a year, so that the third-year dividend payment is $1.33.

The three-year annualized return for a stock that appreciates to $53.25 from $40.00 including dividends received is 12.8%. That is very close to our return estimate of 12.5%, which we calculated by adding the starting dividend yield of 2.5% to the 10% expectation for earnings per share growth. The slight difference between the two returns is due to the timing of dividend payments. (See Table 3.2.)

TABLE 3.2 Base Case

	Year 0	Year 1	Year 2	Year 3
Price = P/E x earnings per share	$40.00	$44.00	$48.40	$53.24
Earnings per share	$4.00	$4.40	$4.84	$5.32
Earnings growth	10.0%	10.0%	10.0%	10.0%
P/E ratio	10	10	10	10
Dividend = dividend payout ratio x earnings	$1.00	$1.10	$1.21	$1.33
Dividend payout ratio = dividend/ earnings per share	25.0%	25.0%	25.0%	25.0%
Dividend yield = dividend/price	2.5%	2.5%	2.5%	2.5%
Earnings growth + dividend yield	12.5%	12.5%	12.5%	12.5%
Annual return = [(new price + dividend)/old price] − 1		12.75%	12.75%	12.75%
3-year annualized return				12.75%
3-year average of earnings growth + dividend yield				12.50%

Let's modify our example slightly. Suppose that all the assumptions stay the same, but at the end of three years investors are willing to pay more for earnings, so the P/E ratio increases to 12x. Under that scenario, the stock price appreciates to $63.89 (i.e., 12 times earnings of $5.32). The three-year annualized return for the stock including dividends is 19.7% instead of 12.7%. Investors' willingness to pay more for earnings has a significant impact on the overall return. (See Table 3.3.)

TABLE 3.3 Increase in Price-to-Earnings Ratio

	Year 0	Year 1	Year 2	Year 3
Price = P/E x earnings per share	$40.00	$44.00	$48.40	$63.84
Earnings per share	$4.00	$4.40	$4.84	$5.32
Earnings growth	10.0%	10.0%	10.0%	10.0%
P/E ratio	10	10	10	12
Dividend = dividend payout ratio x earnings	$1.00	$1.10	$1.21	$1.33
Dividend payout ratio = dividend/earnings per share	25.0%	25.0%	25.0%	25.0%
Dividend yield = dividend/price	2.5%	2.5%	2.5%	2.1%
Earnings growth + dividend yield	12.5%	12.5%	12.5%	12.1%
Annual return = [(new price + dividend)/old price] – 1		12.8%	12.8%	34.8%
3-year annualized return				19.65%
3-year average of earnings growth + dividend yield				12.36%

The Impact of Investor Expectations

At this point you might have picked up on a potential inconsistency. Earlier I shared the most important principle I know when it comes to stock investing: The primary reason to buy an individual stock is if you believe the current price is too low because investors have underestimated what the company's future profit and dividend growth will be. I stated that a stock will only go up in price if the company does better than the consensus view; if the company surprises to the upside. Yet we can clearly see in our example how the stock rose in price as dividends and earnings increased even though investors were willing to pay the same multiple for those earnings. The stock rose in price without any regard to investor expectations. It increased based on the math.

When investors were willing to pay $12 for each $1 of earnings instead of $10, the three-year annualized return went from 12.8% to 19.7%. Why would investors be willing to pay more for each dollar's worth of earnings for this stock? According to conventional financial theory, investors might be willing to pay more because they believe the growth in future dividends and earnings will be higher. Recall that the price of a stock today should equal the present value (i.e., the value in today's dollars) of all future dividends. If investors decide dividend growth will be higher, then they might be willing to pay more for the stock. They will pay a higher multiple of today's earnings, meaning the price-to-earnings ratio will increase. An astute investor might have determined beforehand that the company's growth prospects were better than what was priced into the stock and profited from that knowledge by buying more shares before the P/E multiple increased. Conversely, if the company disappointed and didn't earn as much as expected or there was evidence that earnings growth was slowing, then the stock will fall in price because dividend growth is expected to be lower. Investors will pay less for each dollar of current earnings, and the price-to-earnings ratio will decline.

It all comes down to expectations. At year-end 2017, Amazon stock was selling for $1,169 per share. Its price-to-earnings ratio was 190 times the previous 12 months' earnings of $6.15 per share.[12] Amazon doesn't pay a dividend. This is a stock with lofty expectations. If I had bought some shares of Amazon at the beginning of 2018 and I hold them for five years, my overall return will depend on whether the company's earnings grow, but even more so it will depend on whether earnings grow faster or slower than what investors anticipate. If the earnings grow slower, then the price-to-earnings ratio will fall, and I could suffer a loss on my investment. If earnings come in higher than expected, then I will more than likely earn a profit on my investment. If the earnings grow fast enough, I could earn a profit on my investment even if the P/E ratio declined.

For example, Amazon's annual earnings in 2017 were $6.15 per share. Let's say Amazon grows its earnings by 14% per year over the next five years so that at year-end 2022 its earnings per share are $11.84. If investors are willing to pay 100 times earnings five years from now, Amazon's stock price in five years would be $1,184 (100 x $11.84). That would be close to the $1,169 price at the end of 2017. If investors are willing to pay more than 100 times earnings five years from now, I will make a profit, and if they are willing to pay less, then I will lose money.

There is no way to know whether Amazon will do better or worse than expected, but if we buy a basket of 100 securities with an average P/E ratio of 10 versus a basket of securities with an average P/E ratio of 190, odds are the basket of cheap securities will outperform the more expensive basket, simply because the cheaper basket has such low expectations and will likely surprise investors as earnings come in higher than expected.

In our example, it turns out Amazon earnings jumped by over 220% in 2018 to $20.14 per share. The stock price rose to $1,478 by year-end 2018, an increase of 26%. Given that earnings grew much faster than the stock appreciated, Amazon's P/E ratio at year-end 2018 was 73, down from a P/E ratio of 190 at the start of 2018.[13] (See Table 3.4.)

TABLE 3.4 Amazon Stock

	2017	2023
Price = P/E x earnings per share	$1,169.00	$1,184.13
Earnings per share	$6.15	$11.84
Earnings per share growth	14.0%	14.0%
P/E ratio	190	100

How an Exterminator Can Earn an 80% Return

In this book's Introduction, I shared how an exterminator I hired thought a reasonable return for stocks was 80%. What would have to happen for stocks in terms of the three return drivers to generate that level of performance? Either earnings growth per share would have to be incredibly high, or investors would need to be willing to pay much more for stocks than they do today. In other words, very high cash flow growth or a large change in the cash flow multiple as reflected in the P/E ratio. While that is possible for one stock, as we saw in the Amazon example, it is unlikely for stocks overall, because over the long term the aggregate earnings growth for stocks can't be greater than the overall growth of the economy. Nobel Prize–winning economist Milton Friedman said: "When earnings are exceptionally high, they don't just keep booming. They can't break loose from economic gravity."[14] Let's explore what he means by economic gravity.

How Corporate Profits Are Linked to Economic Growth

Economic growth measures the value of how much a nation produces in goods and services from one period to the next. That output level is called gross domestic product, or GDP. Government statisticians estimate GDP growth by looking at the amount spent by households, businesses, and government from one period to the next or by analyzing the amount of income that households, businesses, and government received.

In other words, business income, which is the same thing as corporate profits, is a factor in estimating GDP growth, which means the faster corporate earnings grow, the faster the economy expands. Yet corporate earnings can only grow if businesses are selling more goods and services or reducing expenses, because earnings equals revenue minus expenses. Business expenses include employee salaries and goods and services bought from other businesses. In aggregate, there is a limit to how much businesses can grow their income by cutting expenses, because eventually the cost reductions with regard to lower salaries would mean households have less money to buy things from businesses, which would impede sales growth and eventually corporate profits.

Likewise, if the elevated earnings growth is from rising sales, then households and businesses have to buy all those additional products and services. If the increased sales come from other businesses, then the businesses buying more products would have higher expenses, which means profits for those businesses are going down. So rising profits from some businesses are offset by lower profits from other businesses. For households to buy the additional products and services, they need higher incomes, which they get from their employers through higher wages, which again would negatively impact corporate profitability as business expenses increase.

These linkages between business and household income and expenses are why Friedman said corporate profits "can't break loose from economic gravity."[15]

The Impact of New Stock Shares and Stock Buybacks

A reasonable assumption for estimating the future returns for stocks is that aggregate corporate sales and earnings will grow at the same rate as the economy. But there is a catch. Overall corporate earnings might grow at the same rate as the economy, but to estimate future stock returns using our three return drivers, the relevant measure is not the growth in overall earnings, but the growth in earnings per stock share. The stock examples above were based on one stock share. But what if companies issue more stock or new companies are formed that issue new stock? That means aggregate corporate profits are spread among more stock shares. If aggregate corporate earnings grow at the same rate as the economy, then the ongoing issuance of stock shares by existing and new companies means overall growth in corporate earnings per share will grow slower than the economy as measured by the increase in nominal GDP.

That is what actually occurs. Over the long term, overall earnings per share growth lags the overall growth in the economy, because the number of stock shares outstanding grows due to new issuance by existing and newly formed companies. By long term, I mean decades. Corporate profits as measured by earnings per share growth can vary significantly from year to year.

Ed Easterling, founder of Crestmont Research, showed that decade by decade there is a positive relationship between nominal GDP growth and corporate profit growth. Yet in each decade from 1960 to 2010, earnings per share growth, while positively correlated with nominal GDP growth, also lagged it. For example, in the 1960s, average U.S. nominal GDP growth was 5.9%, and average U.S. earnings per share growth was 4.4%. From 2000 to 2010, average annual nominal GDP growth was 5.2%, and average earnings per share growth was 4.4%.[16]

The decade beginning in 2010 is a major exception to this pattern. From 2010 to 2017, average U.S. nominal GDP growth was 3.5% per year, while U.S. earnings per share growth averaged 6.5% per year. That certainly seems like a case of corporate profits breaking loose from economic gravity. What happened? Companies have become more profitable. The amount of profit they earn per dollar of sales increased. Meaning their profit margins expanded.[17]

Generally, increased competition should result in above-average profitability returning to more normal levels. That has not been the case this decade. Jeremy Grantham, cofounder of the investment firm GMO, attributes this increase in profitability for U.S. publicly traded companies to a combination of low interest rates, more debt, increased brand power, increased political power, and increased monopoly power.[18]

Another change this decade is the significant increase in companies buying back their stock in the public market. This reduces the number of stock shares outstanding, which leads to an increase in earnings growth per share even if overall corporate earnings stay the same. If aggregate earnings grow at the same rate as the economy, but the number of stock shares is falling, then earnings per share will grow faster than the economy.[19]

The reasons for above-average profitability will continue to be debated. The important takeaway is that if corporate profits are going to continue to grow at a faster rate than the economy, then profit margins need to continue to expand. In other words, companies will need to increase the amount they earn per dollar of sales. Alternatively, earnings per share could continue to grow faster than the economy if the level of stock buybacks remains elevated. If, however, profit margins don't expand but remain at above-average levels, and there is a return to the historical pattern of aggregate stock share counts increasing, then earnings per share growth will again lag nominal GDP growth due to new companies being formed and existing companies issuing new stock shares. Furthermore, if profit margins revert to historical levels, during that transition period, corporate profit growth will significantly lag nominal GDP growth.[20]

Given that earnings per share typically lag nominal GDP growth, a more reasonable assumption for estimating the upside for stocks is that earnings growth per share will track the growth in per capita GDP. Per capita GDP measures the growth of the economy after adjusting for population growth. The amount of output of goods and services produced per person typically lags overall economic growth due to population increases. Academics and practitioners, such as Rob Arnott of Research Affiliates, have found a tight relationship between earnings and dividends growth per share and per capita GDP growth.[21]

HOW TO ESTIMATE RETURNS IN YOUR PORTFOLIO

Our objective as part of answering the question, "What is it?" is to estimate an investment's upside—its expected return. We, of course, won't know for sure what the return will be, but by focusing on the three drivers of performance—our rules of thumb—we can anchor our expectations to reality and not get swept away by fantasies of earning 80% a year like my exterminator.

For example, suppose U.S. bond ETFs are yielding 3.5% as reflected in the SEC yield, and U.S. stock ETFs have a dividend yield of 2.0%. In addition, suppose U.S. real estate investment trust (REIT) ETFs, which are publicly traded companies that own real estate including office buildings, storage facilities, and retail sites, are yielding 4%. If nothing else changes, those yields equal what those investments will return over the next year. In these examples, we are using baskets of securities via ETFs, so their dividend yields tend to change only gradually. For an individual stock or REIT, if the company cuts the dividend, that could dramatically change the dividend yield. (See Table 3.5.)

TABLE 3.5   Estimated Return Examples

Asset	Yield/ Dividend	Cash Flow	Expected Return
U.S. bonds	3.5%	—	3.5%
U.S. stocks	2.0%	4.5%	6.5%
U.S. real estate investment trusts (REITs)	4.0%	4.5%	8.5%

Next we consider our second return driver. Will the cash flow as represented by dividends, interest, or rents grow over time? In the case of the U.S bond ETF, the cash flow could grow if interest rates rise as the bond manager reinvests in higher-yielding bonds, but that higher income will be offset by the price decline due to rising rates.

For stocks, the cash flow will grow over time as earnings per share increase. Let's assume a 4.5% annual increase in profits and cash flow growth for U.S. stocks and REITs. If several years from now investors are willing to pay the same for stocks and REITs as they do today, then a reasonable expectation for U.S. stocks using these assumptions is 6.5% (i.e., the 2.0% dividend yield plus the 4.5% earnings per share growth). For REITs, based on these assumptions, the expected return is 8.5% (i.e., 4.0% dividend yield plus 4.5% cash flow per share growth).

The biggest wild card is whether investors will be willing to pay the same for that cash flow several years from now as they do today. If they are not, then the overall return will be lower or higher than these sample estimates for U.S. stocks and REITs. If they are willing to pay more for the cash flow, then the returns will be higher than these estimates.

Admittedly, developing expected return assumptions for stocks and other asset classes using these rules of thumb can be time consuming. While dividend yields and the P/E ratio for the overall stock market are readily available from index providers such as MSCI, determining the earnings per share growth rate is more challenging. The World Bank provides historical data such as real per capita GDP, to which we can then add an expected inflation assumption to approximate the earnings growth per share, but the extent to which continued stock buybacks will allow earnings per share to grow faster than nominal per capita GDP growth is uncertain.[22]

Rather than calculate your own expected return assumptions, there are a number of investment organizations such as Research Affiliates[23] and GMO[24] that make their asset allocation assumptions available to the general public. These firms use a similar approach to developing their return assumptions as outlined in this chapter.

A MORE REASONABLE FINANCIAL PLAN

My listener's financial planner determined that the listener could retire today if he was able to earn 7.6% per year on his existing assets, but the planner derived the return estimates using historical performance. Let's apply a more realistic forward-looking return assumption of 6.5% for stocks and 2.2% for bonds, based on conditions when the planner compiled the plan in 2017. If the assets are invested 71% in stocks and 29% in bonds, the revised long-term expected return is 5.3%. Those are more solid numbers on which to base a financial plan. Moreover, they likely mean my listener will have to continue working for another decade or more instead of retiring at age 41.

Now that you have rules of thumb for estimating an investment's upside, you have a basis for evaluating the investment assumptions used by financial planners or other practitioners. You will stop and question how someone promising extraordinarily high returns came up with those assumptions. The hope is that you will have the resolve and confidence not to blindly follow the crowd in participating in the latest investment fad, but instead will anchor your return expectations to reasonable levels as you compare various investment options.

CHAPTER SUMMARY

- Using historical returns as the basis for estimating the upside or expected return for an asset class is dangerous, as the conditions that contributed to those historical returns might not be present in the future.

- Rules of thumbs are simple patterns we can follow that are derived from underlying principles without needing to be an expert.

- The rules of thumb for determining an investment's expected return are based on three performance drivers: cash flow, cash flow growth, and the potential change in what investors will pay for the cash flow in the future.

- The best estimate of the expected return for a bond fund or ETF over a seven-year or greater holding period is its current SEC yield or yield to maturity. In the case of high-yield bonds, the SEC yield should be reduced by at least 2.6% to account for potential defaults.

- Duration measures how sensitive a bond opportunity will be to fluctuating interest rates in the short to intermediate term. The greater the duration, the greater the price decline if interest rates rise.

- Prevailing interest rates are based on investors' expectations regarding inflation, future short-term interest rates, and the additional compensation that investors demand for uncertainty regarding those expectations.

- When an individual stock generates an extremely high return, it is because the cash flow grew tremendously or investors were willing to pay much more for existing cash flow.

- The return for a diversified basket of stocks, such as what are available through a broad-based ETF, will rarely exceed double digits over the long term, because the growth in the cash flow cannot exceed the growth rate of the overall economy.

- Applying the rules of thumb for estimating an investment return helps us stay grounded and not get caught up in the latest investment fad promising easy riches.

4

What Is the Downside?

Rules of Thumb for Evaluating Risk

THE TEN QUESTIONS

1. What is it?
2. Is it investing, speculating, or gambling?
3. What is the upside?
4. **What is the downside?**
5. Who is on the other side of the trade?
6. What is the investment vehicle?
7. What does it take to be successful?
8. Who is getting a cut?
9. How does it impact your portfolio?
10. Should you invest?

QUESTION FOUR: WHAT IS THE DOWNSIDE?

The downside of an investment consists of its maximum potential loss and the personal financial harm caused by that loss. When evaluating an investment's downside, the goal is to avoid irreparable financial harm rather than to avoid any loss at all. If you rule out any possibility of a loss in your investing, then you are probably reducing risk too much, and your portfolio might not keep pace with inflation.

After I graduated from high school, I worked for a year at the Netherland Plaza Hotel in downtown Cincinnati. The hotel had just reopened after a major restoration, bringing it to its former Art Deco glory. I lined up with hundreds of other potential job applicants, and after several interviews I was offered employment as a hotel steward. After I started, I learned that hotel stewards wash dishes and mop kitchen floors.

As part of my dishwashing duties, I operated a large automatic dishwasher in the hotel's main restaurant kitchen. My job required me to clear the server trays stacked with dirty dishes as fast as possible, putting the plates and glasses in racks before shoving the racks into the machine. If I didn't move quickly, the table where the bussers set their trays filled up, disrupting the flow of the restaurant. I learned to rapidly dump any liquid from the glasses and place them in the plastic racks overhead. When a rack was full, I shoved it into the dishwasher. I soon discovered that champagne glasses with their narrow necks and delicate sides don't react well to speed. I broke at least a half dozen champagne glasses before I learned to slow down when placing them in a rack. Champagne glasses need stability. The more volatile our movements, the more likely the glasses are to break.

In investing, volatility measures how much a security or asset class deviates from its expected or average return. Cash exhibits very little volatility, as its price from day to day varies little; whereas stocks are much more volatile, because they can exhibit large price swings.

We saw in the previous chapter that when evaluating the attractiveness of an investment opportunity, we need to understand its expected return (i.e., its upside), which is based on three performance drivers: cash flow, cash flow growth, and the potential change in what investors will pay for the cash flow in the future. Investments rise or fall in price as investors reassess future cash flow growth or what they are willing to pay for those cash flows. That constant reassessment leads to volatility. As investors, we don't mind upside volatility when investor reassessment leads to above-average returns. It is the downside volatility that we fear. Before we undertake any investment, we need to answer the question, "What is the downside?" How much could we lose if things don't go as planned? We will see in this chapter that the downside of an investment is a function of not only its potential loss, but also the personal harm caused by the loss.

NAVIGATING THE GLOBAL FINANCIAL CRISIS

Like many of you, I will never forget the six months spanning September 2008 through March 2009 when it appeared the financial system and global economy would completely collapse. During that time, we were reminded of how severe the downside of risk assets, such as stocks and high-yield bonds, could be. I was working as an institutional investment advisor and money manager. My clients were fearful, my partners were worried, and I spent weeks walking around in disbelief.

On September 15, 2008, the investment bank Lehman Brothers filed for bankruptcy—the largest bankruptcy in history. I was in San Diego for a client meeting and happened to get upgraded to the presidential suite at the San Diego Westin hotel. There amid a grand piano, large conference table, and numerous couches and chairs, I watched the financial carnage on television as the U.S. stock market fell close to 5% that day.

"You have to throw out the history books because there's really nothing to compare this to," said Jim Dunigan, chief investment officer at PNC Advisors. He continued, "Any speculation as to what inning we're in becomes difficult because each step of the way seems to bring another drop."[1]

Art Hogan, chief market strategist for Jefferies & Co., said, "We've never witnessed this before. There's no road map for this."[2]

A worried friend and coworker called me at my hotel to ask how I thought this would play out. I told him the same thing I said the next day to the finance committee members of my law school client: that the economy and markets would eventually rebound. A month later in October, I reiterated that point in my firm's third-quarter 2008 market commentary: "We believe this bear market will end, just as all bear markets eventually end. We also believe there are more embedded positive surprises in asset classes purchased during periods of high fear than there are negative surprises."

Why did I believe that? What would the catalyst be for a return to normality? I continued: "When you hold a portfolio comprised of thousands of securities and invest with managers that individually hold hundreds of bonds or hundreds of stocks, the catalyst is capitalism itself and the resiliency of our free market system. The catalyst is the human tendency to shift from greed to fear and back to greed. We expect economic growth to return, fear to subside, and that investors will bid up the value of undervalued asset classes just as they always have." With regard to our investing rules of thumb, we expected that cash flow growth would resume and that investors would again pay reasonable valuations for those cash flow streams.

I believed that, but I had no way of knowing when it would happen. Later in October I wrote in my journal: "This year equity markets are down 50% and the [investment] product I manage is down 30%. I had planned on leaving my company at the end of 2010 with a significant amount of capital. Now I worry the whole thing will implode due to lost clients. None have left and we shall see, but we are preparing for the worst."

What I found so incongruent about the financial collapse is everything still looked the same. There was still the bustle of cars and people on the street below my San Diego hotel room. Later that fall, I walked through the airport in Houston the day of a particularly brutal stock market sell-off. I glanced at my fellow travelers and thought: "They don't act any different. Everything seems so normal."

Yet financial markets were far from normal. From the market peak on October 31, 2007, to the market bottom on March 9, 2009, global stocks as measured by the MSCI All Country World Index fell 58%, with most of those losses occurring between September 2008 and March 2009.[3] The MSCI Emerging Markets Stock Index fell 65% from October 29, 2007, to October 27, 2008.[4] U.S. stocks fell 55% during the bear market.[5] High-yield bonds fell more than 30% as spreads relative to U.S. Treasuries widened dramatically.[6]

Two asset classes that provided safety during this market turmoil were cash and U.S. government bonds, which generated positive returns as investors flocked to those safe havens.

WHAT IS RISK?

Traditional financial theory equates risk with volatility, specifically the degree of variability or movement around the average or expected return. Elroy Dimson, an emeritus professor of finance at the London Business School, has a broader definition of risk that I like. He defines risk as "more things can happen than will happen."[7] The list of things that could potentially happen, both good and bad, is much longer than the list of what actually will happen. As humans, we contemplate this wide range of potential outcomes, acknowledge there are outcomes we haven't considered (i.e., surprises), and then act based on what we expect will happen.

Economic historian Peter L. Bernstein wrote that risk management "should be a process of dealing with the consequences of being wrong"[8] in our expectations. Risk management is especially focused on minimizing the harm and pain caused by negative outcomes. An investment or some other endeavor we are contemplating is more risky if there is a wide range of potential outcomes and the harm caused by being wrong in our expectations is great. Something is less risky if there is a narrow range of potential outcomes and the harm caused by being wrong in our expectations is small.[9]

For example, short-term U.S. government bonds are less risky than stocks since there is a narrower range of potential outcomes for these short-term bonds because their default risk is extremely low and they are less sensitive to interest rate changes. Meanwhile, stocks can fall more than 50% in a downturn, as they did during the global financial crisis of 2008 and 2009.

There is a linkage between volatility and losses. More volatile investments have a wider range of expected returns, which means they are more likely to have some of those returns be negative, resulting in losses. Risk, however, is more than just the absolute loss. It is the personal harm caused by the loss. A 50% decline in stocks could be devastating for an individual who was planning to use the money for a down payment on a house or for retirement at the end of the year. Whereas if the stocks are part of a young investor's meager retirement savings, a 50% decline would be much less harmful.

To repeat, the downside of an investment is a function of its potential loss and the personal harm caused by the loss. For most individuals, investment outcomes are asymmetrical; the harm caused by a loss is more devastating than the benefit from a similar-sized gain. For example, compare how your lifestyle would be affected by a 20% pay cut versus a 20% salary increase. For most of us, a 20% cut would harm us more than the benefits we would get from a 20% raise. But if our income was cut 40%, the harm would not be linear. It would not be twice as bad as a 20% cut, but worse. It would be nonlinear, because at that point we might not be able to pay our bills, and we might be forced to file bankruptcy. In this regard, many of us are like the champagne glasses I broke as a dishwasher.

Big increases in downside volatility could financially break us, just as volatile movements can break fragile glassware.

Risk Tolerance

Not only does the financial harm caused by losses increase exponentially as the losses deepen, but our personal behavior changes. I know investors who have never returned to the stock market after the 2008 financial crisis. A financial advisor would say these investors have low financial risk tolerance. They don't like the uncertainty that comes from investing in more volatile asset classes. John Grable, University of Georgia professor of financial planning, defines risk tolerance as someone's "willingness to engage in risky behavior in which possible outcomes can be negative."[10]

It is common for financial planners to ask potential clients to fill out a questionnaire to help assess their financial risk tolerance. These risk tolerance questionnaires are then used to determine the level of exposure to more volatile asset classes such as stocks. There are a number of problems with these standard risk questionnaires.

Carrie H. Pan and Meir Statman highlighted some of these in their research.[11] They point out that risk tolerance changes based on our circumstances, market conditions, recent experiences, and even the pool of assets being evaluated. Periods of high returns for stocks lead some investors to believe stocks are a high-return, low-risk asset class, so these investors express a willingness to accept more risk following those periods. Likewise, after a market crash like the one in 2008, some investors are fearful and express a low tolerance for risk based on their belief that stocks are a low-returning, high-risk asset class. Some of these same investors might have indicated they had a high risk tolerance before the market crash.[12]

Another problem with risk tolerance questionnaires is we tend to segment our investments into different mental accounts based on differing goals. Consequently, our risk tolerance might differ based on the investment in question. An investor's risk tolerance for a college savings fund might be different than for a fund whose goal is to strike it rich if an aggressive investment works out.[13]

Finally, our tolerance for risk might change based on our personal experiences, leading us to adjust our investment portfolio mix. As time passes, we gain investment experience and our financial circumstances change. Those experiences might make us more or less risk tolerant, depending on our investment decisions and the pattern of market returns. Did we save and invest during an extended period of above-average stock returns, or were stocks in an extended downtrend, punctuated with large market losses?

Behavioral Biases in Making Investment Decisions

It is extremely difficult to choose an investment or portfolio mix by estimating our current or future risk tolerance because our appetite for risk changes based on our experiences, current circumstances, and the mental account into which the investment falls. In short, our assessment of, and aversion toward, risk is changeable and biased. Psychologists Daniel Kahneman and Amos Tversky won a Nobel Prize for their groundbreaking research on how humans make decisions. They wrote, "In making predictions and judgments under uncertainty, people . . . rely on a limited number of heuristics which sometimes yield reasonable judgments and sometimes lead to severe and systematic error."[14] Their research showed individuals assess the likelihood of an event occurring by comparing whatever they are judging with some model in their mind. Are current circumstances representative of the mental model? Do they fit an existing pattern? We do this unconsciously, and when we find a match, we feel in our gut that something is likely to happen or play out in a certain way.[15] Then once we have made up our minds that something is likely to happen, it is often difficult to unhinge that determination.[16]

The mental models we conjure up for comparison are often based on something we recently experienced rather than being more reflective of a broader sample set.[17] After suffering through the global financial crisis of 2008, it was not uncommon in subsequent years for investors and pundits to be convinced in their guts that incoming financial and economic data indicated a recession or bear market was imminent. Sometimes when we conduct mental comparisons, our minds don't find a good match. At other times, we too readily find mental matches and determine an event is highly probable when we shouldn't because current circumstances are unique and/or completely random. Finally, when it comes to decision making, we suffer from hindsight bias. Once something happens, we assign much higher probabilities that it was going to happen, not even remembering the low odds we assigned prior.[18]

The ten-question framework detailed in this book can help us overcome or at least be aware of our inherent behavioral biases when making investment decisions. Rather than rely on our gut, we can anchor our upside and downside return expectations to more objective criteria, like the current income stream, a realistic cash flow growth rate that is tied to economic gravity, and the price investors are currently paying for that cash flow.

MAXIMUM DRAWDOWNS AND RECOVERIES

When it comes to an investment's potential downside, rather than latch onto whatever scenario our mind conjures up based on our recent experiences, a more objective approach is to analyze an investment's worst historical decline, which is known as the maximum drawdown, and calculate how many months or years it took the asset to recoup those losses, which is known as the recovery period. We can then estimate how much financial harm we would experience for a given position size if that worst-case scenario came to pass. Financial harm would include having to change our lifestyle, spending, or future plans.

For stock investments via an index mutual fund or ETF, a realistic assumption is a maximum drawdown of 60% with a recovery period of four years. That has been the historical experience, always recognizing that by definition every worst thing that ever happened always exceeded the previous worst case.

Table 4.1 provides estimates of maximum drawdown and recovery periods for the asset classes discussed in this book.

TABLE 4.1　Maximum Drawdown and Recovery by Asset Class

Asset Class	Maximum Drawdown	Months to Recover
U.S and non-U.S. stocks	−60%	48
Real estate investment trusts	−60%	43
U.S. investment-grade bonds	−5%	12
U.S. high-yield bonds	−36%	18
Cash	0%	0

You may have noticed there are no speculative assets, such as commodities or cryptocurrencies, in the table. For speculations where there is no income stream and there is disagreement among investors whether the return will be positive or negative, I assume a worst-case scenario that I will lose all my money (i.e., a 100% maximum drawdown) with no recovery period. When I invest in a family member's start-up, I assume the money is gone. Yes, it might be structured as an investment, but I consider it a gift. Similarly, my speculations in cryptocurrencies, such as Bitcoin, are scaled to a level that if they plummeted to zero and were deemed worthless, I would be unharmed and accepting of the loss.

Assuming a potential 100% loss for speculations might seem extreme, but this stoical approach mentally prepares us for catastrophe and helps us avoid allocating too much of our capital to speculations. The Roman philosopher Seneca in his fourth letter to his friend Lucilius wrote: "No good thing renders its possessor happy, unless his mind is reconciled to the possibility of loss; nothing, however, is lost with less discomfort than that which, when lost, cannot be missed. Therefore, encourage and toughen your spirit against the mishaps that afflict even the most powerful."[19]

THE POTENTIAL DEVASTATING IMPACT OF LARGE PORTFOLIO LOSSES

A large portfolio loss and an extended recovery period can cause significant financial harm to retirees in terms of how long their retirement assets will last. For example, retirees who withdraw 4% from their portfolio in their first year of retirement and then adjust the annual spending amount by the rate of inflation can expect their portfolio to last 44 years, assuming a 5.5% annual portfolio return and 2.5% annual inflation rate. Yet if their portfolio suffers a 40% decline in the tenth year of retirement and it takes four years to recover from the loss, their portfolio will only last 30 years instead of 44 years if they don't reduce the amount they withdraw from their portfolio each year. The reason for this is the annual withdrawal amount as a percentage of the portfolio's value increases from 4.5% to 8.1% given the smaller asset base after the loss. This concept is easier to grasp if you model it via a spreadsheet. You can do that by downloading my retirement spending spreadsheet and watching a video that explains how to use it. You can find those resources at https://moneyfortherestofus.com/tools.

WHY ASSETS FALL IN PRICE

Investments fall in price because investors believe future cash flow growth will be lower or because they are unwilling to pay as much for that future cash flow. What causes investors to constantly adjust their assessment of asset classes, leading to market volatility? One influence is changing interest rates. Financial theory states that the correct price of a stock is the present value of its future dividends. The present value is the price in today's dollars of a future cash flow stream. Another way to describe present value is that it is the value that makes an investor indifferent to receiving cash today or cash in the future.

What would make an investor indifferent to receiving cash today or cash in the future? An investor would be indifferent if the cash delivered a year from now earned a rate of return that met the investor's minimum return requirement. For example, an investor who demands a return of 6% for an investment would be indifferent to receiving $100 today or $106 one year from now since a 6% annual return on a $100 investment equals $6. In this example, the present value of $106 received a year from now is $100. Suppose the yield on relatively risk-free one-year U.S. government bonds went from 2% to 3%. In that case, an investor might then require a return of 7% instead of 6% to hold a risky investment for one year. At a 7% required rate of return, the present value of $106 received one year from now is $99.07. The present value or price in today's dollar fell by just under $1.00 as the investor's required rate of return went from 6% to 7%.

Investors' required rate of return fluctuates as interest rates change, because if rates rise and investors can earn 1% more on risk-free short-term government bonds, then they will require a higher return on risky investments, which can cause the prices of those investments to fall as the higher required rate of return leads to a lower present value of future cash flow streams. We saw in the last chapter that interest rates fluctuate as expected inflation increases or decreases, as the expected path of short-term interest rates changes, or if there is a change in the term premium that investors require to compensate for unanticipated inflation or higher future interest rates.

In addition to changing interest rates, asset prices are volatile as investors assess the impact of the overall economy on future cash flows. A contracting economy can hurt corporate earnings as sales decline. Lower profits potentially mean lower dividend payments to investors, leading to a lower present value of those dividends; hence a falling stock price. In the United States since 1916, ten of the twelve deepest drawdowns for stocks have occurred during economic recessions, with an average decline of 47%, according to data from Ned Davis Research.[20] Mervyn King, former governor of the Bank of England, wrote: "Stock prices move around because investors are trying to cope with an unknowable future. Their judgements about future profits can be highly unstable. This instability is fundamental to a capitalist economy."[21]

Lower corporate profits also make it more difficult for companies to pay interest and principal on outstanding debt. This increases the risk of default, leading investors to demand additional compensation from corporate borrowers in the form of higher yields (i.e., spreads) to compensate for that risk. That results in lower bond prices.

What this means is volatility for stocks and bonds often spikes at the same time the economy slows. There is a clustering effect as periods of relative calm in the financial markets are followed by more turbulent periods, just as the jolt from hitting an air pocket while flying in a plane is usually followed by another one. Volatility increases as investors reassess the prospects of their investments in light of a changing economy.

Investors' constant reassessment of their return requirements and the economic components that drive those returns also impacts corporate behavior with regard to the capital projects and other initiatives they choose to pursue. Harvard finance professor Mihir Desai wrote: "Finance's answer to the question of where value comes from is simple— the capital you're entrusted with has a cost because the people who gave it to you have expectations for returns. . . . Their expected return is your cost of capital. You are a steward of their capital, and the [essential condition] of value creation is you have to *exceed* their expectations and your cost of capital if you want to create value."[22]

When a business such as an airline evaluates a project like purchasing a new airplane or entering a new market, it seeks to generate a return on the project that exceeds its cost of capital, which is the weighted average of the interest rate on its debt and the estimated return requirement for stock investors. If the business consistently implements projects that exceed its cost of capital, then the market valuation as reflected in its stock price increases. Businesses like this create value. These firms give back more than they take. Firms that undertake investment projects whose returns fall short of their financing cost destroy value. Of course, if investors increase their required rates of return for stocks and bonds, the hurdle rate that corporate projects must exceed as reflected in the cost of capital also increases. That means some corporate projects might not get funded, as the cost of capital increases and the projects become less economically viable.

HOW TO MANAGE RISK IN YOUR PORTFOLIO

The downside of an investment is a function of its potential loss and the personal harm caused by the loss. When evaluating an investment's downside, the goal is to avoid irreparable financial harm rather than to avoid any loss at all. Ben Bernanke, former chairman of the Federal Reserve, related how two of his mentors used to say, "If you never miss a plane, you're spending too much time in airports."[23] Bernanke interpreted this to mean, "If you absolutely rule out any possibility of any kind of financial crisis, then you're probably reducing risk too much, in terms of growth and innovation in the economy."[24] From an investing perspective, that airplane metaphor means if you rule out any possibility of a loss in your investing, then you are probably reducing risk too much, and your portfolio might not even keep pace with inflation. That means your portfolio might seem safe, but it is actually losing money on a real or inflation-adjusted basis.

As investors, we have inherent behavioral biases that make it difficult to assess both our risk tolerance and the riskiness of an investment. Consequently, an objective approach to determining an investment's downside is to analyze its maximum drawdown (i.e., its worst historical decline) and its recovery period (i.e., how long it took to recoup losses), and then estimate the financial harm a loss would inflict on us for a given position size. For speculations, such as cryptocurrencies, where there is no income stream, a prudent approach is to assume a maximum drawdown of 100% with no recovery. For retirees, large portfolio losses can be especially devastating. You can see the impact of these losses by downloading my retirement spending spreadsheet and watching a video that explains how to use it. You can find those resources at https://moneyfortherest ofus.com/tools.

Investors who are decades away from retirement are unlikely to suffer irreparable financial harm even if stocks fall 60%, because there is sufficient time for stocks to recover before the money is needed. Consequently, these investors can withstand the volatility of having more of their portfolios invested in stocks, allowing them to benefit from an asset class that has outpaced inflation over the long term.

CHAPTER SUMMARY

- Volatility measures how much a security or asset class deviates from its expected or average return. The greater an investment's volatility, the greater the likelihood it will lose money at some point.

- Volatility tends to cluster, as periods of relative calm in the financial markets are followed by more turbulent periods.

- The downside of an investment is a function of its potential loss and the personal harm caused by the loss. When evaluating an investment's downside, the goal is to avoid irreparable financial harm, not to avoid losses.

- An objective approach to determining an investment's downside is to analyze its maximum drawdown (i.e., its worst historical decline) and its recovery period (i.e., how long it took to recoup losses), and then estimate the financial harm a loss would cause us for a given position size.

- Investments fall in price because investors believe future cash flow growth will be lower or because they are unwilling to pay as much for that future cash flow. Changes in interest rates and economic growth prospects contribute to market volatility.

5

Who Is on the Other Side of the Trade?

Evaluating What the Seller Knows About an Investment

THE TEN QUESTIONS

1. What is it?
2. Is it investing, speculating, or gambling?
3. What is the upside?
4. What is the downside?
5. **Who is on the other side of the trade?**
6. What is the investment vehicle?
7. What does it take to be successful?
8. Who is getting a cut?
9. How does it impact your portfolio?
10. Should you invest?

QUESTION FIVE: WHO IS ON
THE OTHER SIDE OF THE TRADE?

Knowing who is selling us an investment helps us avoid financial instruments where success is dependent on knowing the
future and/or outsmarting other investors.

Investing is not something we do alone. In order to enter a new investment, someone has to sell it to us. The seller could be another investor, or
the seller could be the investment sponsor if it is an investment offering
managed by a professional advisor. This chapter looks at what to consider
when interacting with other investors, particularly what does the seller
know that we might not.

Before I began work as an investment advisor, I spent three years as
a financial analyst with a leasing company in Dayton, Ohio. After about
18 months with this company, I felt like I knew enough about the math
of leasing to lease a car. We had just bought our first house, money was
tight, and I was tired of having to fix my old pickup truck I drove to work
each day. My goal when I entered the Toyota dealership down the street
from my office was to find and lease a new car with the lowest monthly
payment and least money down. I didn't care what model it was, nor its
color or features. All I cared about was keeping my payment low. That
meant I wanted a new car with a warranty, so I didn't have to pay to fix
the vehicle.

Once I found a car, the dealership's finance manager and I negoti-
ated back and forth, with the sales rep serving as a go-between until the
manager finally invited me back to his office. After he recognized my
familiarity with the economics of leasing, he turned his computer screen
toward me to reveal the details of the deal, including the dealership's cost,
its profit, the interest rate, and the estimated residual value at the end of
three years. At that point, I agreed to lease the car. The dealership's profit

on the transaction was less than $300, and even if there was an additional incentive payment the dealer would eventually receive from Toyota, the manager's transparency in showing me his screen convinced me to sign the lease. I drove out of the dealership in a white Toyota Tercel with large black bumpers. This was the car I would later keep hidden from my investment advisory clients in order to avoid revealing how little money I had. We called the vehicle "the little auto." My monthly lease payment was less than $200.

I was comfortable entering into this lease transaction because I felt like I had enough information to make a sound decision. I knew who I was dealing with, I trusted the Toyota brand, I had transparency on the details of the transaction, and I had a warranty to protect me if the car ran into mechanical issues.

Let's compare this new car transaction with my experience as a "commodities trader" that I shared in Chapter 2. When I entered into an oil futures contract, my order was routed from my broker to the commodity exchange, which acted as the counterparty to both the buyer (me) and the seller of the futures contract. I didn't need to worry about the transaction failing, because the financial resources of the CME Group, the owner of the commodities exchange, backed the transaction. For most transactions involving publicly traded securities such as stocks, ETFs, and bonds, we don't have to worry about the transaction failing. There are usually the financial resources of the broker and the exchange to back the transaction as well as some type of insurance fund to protect investors in case the broker goes bankrupt. When we sell a stock, we can be confident that the transaction will clear and we will get our money.

That's not the case with private transactions. In the case of the Toyota dealership, I trusted the owners would deliver the vehicle to me if I entered into a lease. In addition, I had a lease contract to protect me. But when I sold the car to a private buyer at the end of the lease, I took payment in cash so I didn't have to worry about a check bouncing and not receiving my funds.

Unlike the future price of oil, I was highly confident in the direction of the car's future price. It would definitely fall as the car depreciated, but my downside was limited. I could return the car to Toyota at the end of the lease if it was worth less than the residual value assumed in the lease contract. Or if it was worth more, I could buy the car for the residual value and then sell it to a third party and make a small profit, which is what I ended up doing. With the oil futures contract, I had no insight into how much oil was being produced, refined, stored, or consumed. I didn't know the volume of buy and sell orders or what orders might be waiting to be executed. I was effectively guessing the price would go up. That is why it was a speculation.

WITH WHOM ARE YOU TRADING?

As investors, whenever we contemplate a new investment, we need to answer who is on the other side of the trade. There are two aspects to this transactional knowledge. The first is knowledge of the counterparty. How confident are we that the transaction will go through, and what protections exist if something goes wrong?

For example, there are a number of real estate crowdfunding sites where investors can ostensibly lend to borrowers who use the funds to fix up a house to flip or an apartment to rent. Some investors may not realize they are not really lending to the borrower, so they do not have a security interest in the underlying property if the borrower defaults. The crowdfunding platform is the entity that made the loan to the borrower and has the security interest in the property. The investor actually invested in a mortgage-dependent promissory note issued by the platform. The platform is required to pay on the promissory note as the interest and principal payments are received from the borrower. But if the crowdfunding platform files for bankruptcy, the holders of the mortgage-dependent promissory note have an unsecured liability in the platform. They will wait in line with other unsecured creditors and will be junior in seniority to any senior debt the platform has outstanding. Consequently, there is more counterparty risk with crowdfunding investing platforms than many investors recognize.

The second piece of knowledge relates to what the seller might know about the investment's future price that you or I might not know. A classic example of having an informational edge about the future price of an asset was a thought experiment by the Roman philosopher Cicero. In his volume titled *De Officiis* written in 44 BC, Cicero wrote: "Suppose, for example, a time of dearth and famine at Rhodes, with provisions at fabulous prices; and suppose that an honest man has imported a large cargo of grain from Alexandria and that to his certain knowledge also several other importers have set sail from Alexandria, and that on the voyage he has sighted their vessels laden with grain and bound for Rhodes; is he to report the fact to the Rhodians or is he to keep his own counsel and sell his own stock at the highest market price?"

Cicero goes on to point out that this is a virtuous, upright man. He says, "I am raising the question how a man would think and reason who would not conceal the facts from the Rhodians if he thought it was immoral to do so, but who might be in doubt whether such silence would really be immoral."[1] The merchant had an informational insight regarding order flow. He knew there would be a huge spike in supply when the additional merchant ships arrive. Cicero then shares the discussion between Diogenes of Babylonia and his pupil Antipater, who disagree about whether the merchant should disclose this information that will more than likely impact the future price of grain.[2] Although this is only a thought experiment, it is interesting how the merchant had days or weeks to decide what to do with this informational edge because the knowledge that could impact prices in the form of the ships laden with grain moved so slowly.

FINANCIAL MARKETS ARE INCREASINGLY MORE COMPETITIVE

Information that impacts market prices moves more quickly today—not weeks or days, but milliseconds. I mentioned I was unsuccessful in my attempt to trade commodity futures because I had no insight into the demand and supply of the underlying commodities, and I had no data on order flow. Ten to twenty years ago there were hundreds of commodity hedge funds that had that kind of information and could use it for their profit. Now the pool of hedge funds trading on fundamental information is shrinking because trading in commodities futures is dominated by computers running quantitative trading algorithms that constantly evolve based on artificial intelligence. Data from the Commodity Futures Trading Association shows automated trading accounts for 80% of foreign currency futures, 70% of stocks, and over 50% for energy-related futures.[3]

Marwan Younes, chief investment officer of commodity hedge fund Massar Capital Management, said: "Twenty years ago, if you were to talk to a commodity manager and ask him why should we invest with you, the typical answer would be, 'Well I have all these networks of people and call them for any information I need.' Today, pointing to proprietary information to be your edge is really dubious."[4]

Jonathan Goldberg, founder of the energy-focused hedge fund BBL Commodities, said: "Trading exclusively on information that everyone has access to, such as government data and inventory reports, is a fool's errand. 'You're not going to be able to click quicker than a machine—that is like saying you can deliver a package quicker than Amazon. . . . Maybe you could have 10 years ago, but you can't now.'"[5]

Yet some individual investors continue to try to compete with institutional traders. I once met a furniture salesman who was more excited about trading commodity futures and foreign currencies than he was about selling furniture. He was 65 and had worked at the furniture company for 14 years. He had never participated in his employer's defined contribution plan. This man could effectively earn an immediate 100% return on the portion of his contributions that were matched by his employer. However, he said he hadn't participated because stocks were risky, and he could lose money investing in them. Now his goal was to be able to retire by age 70, and he had paid a trading academy $23,000 to teach him how to trade commodity futures and foreign currencies. The man said, "You have to invest in yourself." He mentioned he had the opportunity to pay $50,000 to join the academy's mastermind level where he could get individual mentoring, but he went with the "less expensive" package.

I attended a four-hour workshop at the trading academy the furniture salesman had joined so I could better understand how the academy was able to convince a man with little investment experience to pay such a large sum to learn how to trade. The academy was very up front that traders can quickly lose all their capital because options and futures are highly leveraged in that gains and losses are magnified due to the small amount of money required to enter into a trade. The way to be a successful trader, the instructors at the academy said, was to exit the losing trades quickly and let the winners run. They emphasized that if traders make significantly more money on the winning trades than they lose on losing trades, then they need only be right a little over half the time. They shared how to do that in their U.S. patent for their trading process. It states, "Operating under the assumption that trading in most markets is a zero sum game (winners win at the expense of losers losing), it is important to identify the mistakes that other traders typically make in markets so that these can be exploited."[6] The patent makes clear that it is novice traders who are exploited and lose to institutional traders. Most of these novice traders are individual investors who trade on "nothing more than gut feel,"[7] or they buy "after a rally in price"[8] at price points where the supply of willing sellers (usually institutions and trading bots) is greater than the supply of willing buyers. Given there are more willing sellers than buyers, the price drops and the novice investor loses money.[9]

ACTIVE MANAGER UNDERPERFORMANCE

It is disheartening how many novice investors are exploited in this way. That is why it is so important to understand who is on the other side of the trade and whether the investment manager or trader on the other side knows more than we do about what could impact the price. For active managers and traders to consistently outperform the market or each other, they have to be better at security selection than other active managers and traders. Individuals and institutional investors who allocate to these active managers and traders also have the daunting task of determining beforehand which managers are skilled at security selection. Rob Arnott, founder of the investment research firm Research Affiliates, said, "When you choose an active manager. . . . you'd better have a good answer to the question if this active manager is a winner, because there's a loser on the other side of their trades, who's the loser and why are they a willing loser?"[10] Having spent much of my investment career trying to identify skilled active managers, I can attest that this is not an easy task, particularly because skilled managers go through periods of underperformance and unskilled managers can get lucky with extended periods of outperformance. S&P conducts an annual persistence study that shows relatively few managers stay consistently in the top half of their peer group in terms of performance.[11]

Malcom Gladwell shared this statistical thought experiment that demonstrates how lucky investors can generate performance that makes them look skilled. The experiment starts with a sample of 10,000 investment managers, and by chance, half of them make money and half do not in any given year. Gladwell wrote: "Suppose that every year the losers were tossed out, and the game replayed with those who remained. At the end of five years, there would be three hundred and thirteen people who had made money in every one of those years, and after ten years there would be nine people who had made money every single year in a row—all out of pure luck."[12]

Fifty years ago, it was easier for an active manager to select outperforming securities, because it was primarily individual investors on the other side of the trade who prematurely sold the securities that ended up performing so well. But now individuals get most of their stock and bond exposure through mutual funds and exchange-traded funds, some passive and some active. That means active professional managers are competing among themselves to be the superior stock and bond selectors, and more and more of those security selectors are quantitative trading algorithms

Each year, S&P Dow Jones Indices produces scorecards comparing active stock managers with market indices that approximate the managers' particular investment strategy. These S&P Indices Versus Active (SPIVA) reports consistently show that most active managers around the world underperform passively managed benchmarks net of fees. For example, for the 15 years ending December 31, 2018, 92% of U.S. large-cap stock funds trailed the S&P 500 Index, and 97% of small-company funds trailed the S&P 600 Index, a measure of U.S. small-company stocks.[13] Of course as investors, we can't invest directly in a market index. We have to invest in an index mutual fund or ETF. Morningstar produces a semiannual report that compares the performance of active managers relative to a composite of passively managed funds. The performance of both the active and passive strategies is reduced by investment costs such as management fees. The report shows that the vast majority of active managers underperform a comparable passively managed strategy net of fees over 10-, 15-, and 20-year periods.[14] More sobering is these long-term studies by S&P and Morningstar only include the active managers that were still managing money after 10, 15, and 20 years. There are many that underperformed and shut down or merged, and so their track records are not included in the studies. Had they survived, the percentage of underperforming managers would be even higher.

At least in the stock and bond markets, over a long enough period of time, all investors, both active and passive, will earn a positive return. That's because stock returns are driven by dividends and dividend growth, which is linked to the growth in the economy, while bond returns are driven by interest income. That's not the case in the commodities futures market or in the foreign exchange market. In the commodities futures market, every trader that initiates a trade in which he expects the future price of oil will rise is matched with a trade from someone who expects the future price of oil will fall. Since every winning trade is offset by a losing trade, the average return across all market participants is zero. The only guaranteed positive return in the futures market is the interest income investors receive on the money they are required to keep in their brokerage account to offset any losses they incur in the futures market. These funds held at the brokerage are known as a maintenance margin.

The foreign exchange market also has an expected return of zero before fees. Foreign exchange is the largest financial market in the world, with more than $5 trillion of transactions on the average day. Major players in the foreign exchange market include governments, businesses conducting trade, hedge funds, and individuals. The foreign exchange market is an over-the-counter market in that transactions take place on various electronic platforms or between banks and market participants rather than on a centralized exchange. For example, a trader might speculate that the U.S dollar will be worth less relative to the euro, so she exchanges dollars for euros. Meanwhile, an entity on the other side of the trade exchanges euros for dollars. If the dollar weakens, the trader will earn a profit when she converts the euros back to dollars, but the entity who converted the euros to dollars will have lost money. In the foreign exchange market, for every winner there is a loser. The net return across all participants is zero. And after commissions or fees charged by banks or other trading platforms, the net return is negative.

We learned in Chapter 2 that buying an asset with a negative expected return is a form of gambling. Given the zero-sum game nature of the commodities futures and foreign exchange markets, it is extremely unlikely that you or I will be able to profit from knowing something other investors don't. Actually, I already know I wouldn't be successful at trading futures contracts and foreign currencies, because I have tried and failed. That's why I stick with asset classes that have a positive expected return, because there is cash flow and growth in that cash flow over time. If we want to be successful traders (as opposed to investors), we need to participate in a financial market where securities have a positive expected return and where the majority of investors are individuals rather than sophisticated institutions and algorithms. The only market I am aware of that fits that description is closed-end funds, an investment vehicle we will explore in the next chapter.

The investing math and data from reporting services like SPIVA[15] and Morningstar[16] clearly show that outperforming the stock market by identifying stocks that are mispriced is extremely difficult to do. Only stocks that are undervalued in that their current price is lower than the present value (i.e., the price in today's dollars) of their future dividends will perform better than the overall market. These are the stocks that surprise to the upside by doing better than the consensus view of market participants. Conversely, stocks that do worse than the consensus opinion will underperform the market.

ARE MARKETS EFFICIENT?

Here's a question to consider: If it is difficult for individuals and professional investors to identify and profit from mispriced securities, does that then mean stocks and other financial assets are always priced correctly? I don't think so. The collective wisdom of market participants can be wrong.

When I studied finance in graduate school and as an undergrad, I was taught the efficient market hypothesis. This theory was conveyed less as a hypothesis and more as doctrine that wasn't to be questioned. The efficient market hypothesis was developed by Paul A. Samuelson and Eugene Fama, both of whom won the Nobel Prize in Economics. In 1965, Eugene Fama wrote:

An "efficient" market is defined as a market where there are a large number of rational, profit-maximizers actively competing, with each trying to predict future market values of individual securities, and where important current information is almost freely available to all participants.

In an efficient market, competition among the many intelligent participants leads to a situation where, at any point in time, actual prices of individual securities already reflect the effects of information based both on events that have already occurred and on events which, as of now, the market expects to take place in the future.[17]

In other words, there are no mispriced securities, according to the strongest form of this theory. Every stock reflects its intrinsic value, the present value of its future dividend stream. Why spend time trying to pick individual securities if everything is already reflected in the price? We might as well invest in passive index funds rather than seek out active managers.

That's what I was taught, although I only sort of believed it. After graduate school I still researched and invested in individual stocks for my own portfolio. Some lessons have to be learned by doing. When I became an institutional investment advisor, I spent a great deal of time conducting due diligence on active stock and bond managers, many of whom had outperformed the market. About seven years into my investment career, I got the idea of building a stock portfolio composed of the top ten holdings of our top recommended stock managers. This would be a portfolio of the highest-conviction stockholdings from our highest-conviction investment firms, firms that had outperformed the market and that we recommended to our clients. I spent several months back-testing this strategy, convinced this inspired idea would make millions for our clients (as well an attractive income stream for my partners and me), while allowing me to cut back on my extensive business travel and spend more time with my family. How could it fail? An 80-stock portfolio of the best of the best.

It didn't work. I constructed portfolios using risk management software from Barra to optimize the weights of each holding in order to make sure the portfolio didn't exhibit too much tracking error. Tracking error measures how much a portfolio deviates from a target index. When I compared the performance of the portfolios I built with the Russell 3000 Index, a measure of the U.S. stock market, my portfolios consistently underperformed the index after subtracting the estimated management fee.

How could this be? Either my colleagues and I were lousy at selecting stock managers, or something else was going on. I later determined that much of the outperformance I saw from managers was not due to their skill in selecting individual stocks. Rather, their excess returns resulted from particular biases or factors built into their portfolios, such as a higher dividend yield, lower price-to-earnings ratio, or additional credit risk. Factors are broad, persistent drivers of return.[18] For example, fixed-income managers can outperform a bond benchmark such as the Bloomberg Barclays Aggregate Bond Index by allocating more to higher-yielding corporate bonds, including non-investment-grade bonds. The excess return has less to do with the performance of any given bond, and more to do with the incremental yield received to compensate for the higher risk of default. In my portfolio experiment, by reducing tracking error relative to the broad stock market, I had inadvertently reduced or eliminated the factors that had driven the specific managers' outperformance. By combining the holdings of numerous managers with different styles such as value, growth, and momentum, I effectively neutralized the factors, resulting in a portfolio that stylistically was similar to the overall market, but with higher fees and trading costs. Hence, the portfolio underperformed.

After that disappointing exercise, I realized that rather than pay active managers for exposure to a given factor, such as a value bias, I could construct a portfolio of exchange-traded funds comprising thousands of underlying securities that emphasized areas of the financial markets that had the most compelling valuations. These were areas that had the highest expected return at any given time, such as emerging markets or small-company value stocks, because they were selling for prices that were below their historical valuations. These were areas where investors refused to pay more for future cash flow growth, often because they were overly pessimistic or fearful. I backtested this approach, and a partner and I put up the money to create the performance track record. The product was successful and eventually attracted nearly $2 billion in client assets, although it was a rocky ride at times such as during the 2008 global financial crisis.

The launch of this advisory product was based on my personal experience that the stock market seems to be micro efficient in that it is difficult for active managers to take advantage of security mispricings, but there are also periods when the market is macro inefficient in that valuations seem to disconnect from reality. Bubbles form, or asset classes become extraordinarily inexpensive. I later learned this concept of micro efficiency and macro inefficiency is called Samuelson's dictum after Nobel Prize–winning economist Paul A. Samuelson who first hypothesized about it.[19]

At this point in my investment career, I had already lived through the rise and collapse of the dot-com bubble, a period that began in the late 1990s when internet-related stocks soared in price and reached extreme valuations. Even though I knew that it was extremely difficult for active managers to outperform the market, I also knew that market participants could collectively drive security prices to levels well beyond reasonable expectations. In other words, the combination of investors' greed and their fear of missing out was so powerful at times that they were willing to pay exorbitant sums for expected cash flow growth. During other periods, fear of losses caused investors to dump assets indiscriminately, pushing valuations well below their historical averages. I realized that investors as a group could be wrong and that securities could be mispriced even if it was difficult to determine exactly which security.

In March 2000, shortly before the dot-com bubble burst, my advisory firm published a paper I wrote titled "Should Fiduciaries Overweight Growth Stocks in Investment Portfolios?" I worked on that paper for several months, spending hours in the library of my alma mater digging through academic journals, trying to understand whether the investment world had indeed changed. I had only been an investment professional for five years, all during a raging bull market. Maybe it really was different this time.

From my research I learned the long-term performance of stocks is driven by the three performance drivers I have already described in this book: dividends, earnings growth, and what investors are willing to pay for those earnings. Every stock has an implied embedded growth rate priced into it. Investors are willing to pay a premium for stocks with higher expected earnings growth than for stocks whose earnings are slower and more erratic. But here is the key. A stock will only outperform the market if its actual earnings growth exceeds the earnings growth rate already priced into the stock. Outperformance is not due to a company growing its earnings faster than other companies. All that matters is whether the company grows its earnings faster than what investors have assumed the earnings growth rate will be. Here is how I put it in the paper:

> Certainly the rise of the Internet and other New Economy technological advances has had a profound impact on capital markets and on our daily lives. Without a doubt, growth stocks deserve higher valuations than old economy value stocks since their earnings grow at a faster rate. Nevertheless, fiduciaries that overweight growth stocks in their portfolios must understand that their wager is not whether technology related growth stocks will change the world as we know it. The answer to that question is a definite yes. Fiduciaries who overweight growth stocks are wagering that Wall Street analysts and other market participants are currently underestimating the earnings growth rates of these

New Economy stocks, whereas historically they have overesti-mated earnings growth. If investors are willing to make the above bet, then the relevant question is. . . . does the potential benefit of being correct more than offset the penalty of being wrong?[20]

ADAPTIVE MARKETS

I didn't propose a new theory for what I was experiencing as an invest-ment advisor, but Andrew W. Lo, professor of finance at the MIT Sloan School of Management, did. The theory he developed that expands upon the efficient market hypothesis is called the adaptive markets hypothesis. The theory states that in many environments markets are indeed efficient in that securities are priced correctly. At other times, the environment changes enough that the heuristics, or rules of thumb, investors use to make portfolio decisions are suboptimal.[21] Lo writes:

> The wisdom of the crowds depends on the errors of individual investors canceling each other out. But if we all exhibit certain behavioral patterns that are constantly irrational in the same way, sometimes the errors don't cancel out. If you use a defective scale that's biased upwards, averaging your weight across multiple readings on the scale won't give you a more accurate measure of your weight. . . .
>
> . . . While arbitrage and profit motive can exploit a misjudg-ment, they still rely on the ability of investors to recognize when a mistake has taken place. In many cases, this expectation is sim-ply unrealistic. The history of markets is filled with "rational" investors going wrong with utter confidence in the soundness of their judgment until brought down by information just beyond their range of consideration or understanding.[22]

Lo suggests that collectively market participants can be wrong, resulting in a systematic overvaluation or undervaluation of asset classes or subsegments of the market. The adaptive market hypothesis labels this behavior as suboptimal, rather than purely irrational, because the heuristic or frame of reference investors use no longer fits the market environment.[23] Lo gives the example of a great white shark on a beach. The shark obviously isn't adapted to the new environment, leading to suboptimal behavior.[24]

Market participants can collectively be wrong, because they are acting under conditions of extreme uncertainty. To take action, investors construct narratives or stories about what they think will happen. David Tuckett, director of the Centre for the Study of Decision-Making Uncertainty at University College of London, said: "The prices of financial assets cannot be set by fundamentals—which are unknown and in [the] future unknowable—they are set by stories about fundamentals—specifically the stories which market consensus at any one moment judges true. Moreover, because the most popular stories judged true can change significantly more quickly than fundamentals, asset valuations can change very rapidly indeed."[25]

Tuckett points out there are times when these stories become completely unrealistic, as they did during the dot-com bubble and tulip mania. Participants chase after what he labels "phantastic objects," which are highly exciting ideas, people, or things that fulfil our deepest desires and promise compelling gains. These idealized objects are so attractive in our minds that they repel any doubt that things might not go as planned. They can lead investors to take excessive risk by allocating a huge amount of their net worth to highly concentrated speculations, such as cryptocurrencies, that are deemed a sure bet.

Our ten-question framework helps us stay grounded and not fall victim to phantastic objects, including investment professionals and strategies that promise outsized rewards with little or no risk. As we evaluate the upside and downside of a particular investment and what has to happen for the investment to be successful, we can craft more reasonable narratives that make room for doubt and keep us from becoming overly confident. In addition, as part of our research we can seek out credible sources that provide narratives that may contradict our views.

HOW TO BALANCE ACTIVE AND PASSIVE INVESTING IN YOUR PORTFOLIO

Answering the question, "Who is on the other side of the trade?" helps us to avoid losses by identifying counterparty risk that might lead to a failed trade because another party in the transaction doesn't keep its side of the deal. In addition, considering "who is on the other side of the trade" helps us to avoid financial situations such as trading foreign currencies that, in order to make a profit, require us to be smarter or more knowledgeable than the entity selling us the asset. Prudent investors focus on investment opportunities that have positive expected returns that aren't dependent on outsmarting other investors. That focus leads many investors, including me, to primarily use low-cost passive index funds or ETFs in their portfolios. These passive vehicles seek to match the return of an area of the market in contrast to active vehicles that seek to outperform a market segment through security selection.

The use of passive index funds does not mean investors should be passive in all areas of their investing. In his book, Andrew Lo asks—and answers—the provocative question: "Must passive investing always accept risk passively, and never have the benefits of active management? The answer is no."[26] Part of being a portfolio manager is actively allocating to the areas of the market that are most compelling with regard to the expected return and valuation and avoiding areas where investors are overly optimistic, suggesting future returns will be lower. That is risk management. Risk management is not about predicting the future. It is, as hedge fund manager Ray Dalio says, reacting "appropriately to the information available at each point of time."[27] That doesn't mean we make daily, weekly, or even monthly changes to our portfolios. It simply means we stay aware of the market environment, pay attention to the stories investors are telling themselves, and prudently make asset allocation adjustments when appropriate.

CHAPTER SUMMARY

- Answering the question, "Who is on the other side of the trade?" helps us identify counterparty risk that might lead to losses due to a failed trade because another party in the transaction doesn't keep its side of the deal.

- Answering who is on the other side of the trade also helps us avoid investments where financial success is dependent on knowing the future and/or outsmarting other investors.

- The data from performance reporting services shows that outperforming the stock market by identifying stocks that are mispriced is extremely difficult to do; most active managers underperform, and those that do outperform have a difficult time sustaining that outperformance relative to peers.

- While it is difficult to identify individual mispriced securities, investors in aggregate can still be wrong, resulting in a systematic overvaluation or undervaluation of asset classes or subsegments of the market.

- Portfolio and risk management involves actively allocating to the areas of the market that are most compelling in terms of the expected return and valuation, and avoiding areas where investors are overly optimistic, suggesting future returns will be lower.

6

What Is the Investment Vehicle?

Evaluating Exchange-Traded Funds, Mutual Funds, and Other Investment Securities

---

THE TEN QUESTIONS

1. What is it?
2. Is it investing, speculating, or gambling?
3. What is the upside?
4. What is the downside?
5. Who is on the other side of the trade?
6. **What is the investment vehicle?**
7. What does it take to be successful?
8. Who is getting a cut?
9. How does it impact your portfolio?
10. Should you invest?

QUESTION SIX: WHAT IS THE INVESTMENT VEHICLE?

An investment vehicle is an instrument, product, or container that houses a particular investment strategy. Before investing,. we should be able to explain an investment vehicle's attributes including the expected return, the risk in terms of the potential maximum drawdown, liquidity, fees, structure, and pricing.

A listener to my podcast asked me about an investment with which he was unfamiliar. His father, who was 97 at the time, had recently fallen and was recovering from hip replacement surgery. The father asked his son to help him with his taxes. Several of the tax forms listed investments with long, confusing names, so the listener asked his father's broker about them. The broker forwarded some information about the investments, which my listener then sent to me in case I wanted to discuss them on my show.

One of the investments was labeled an "autocallable contingent income note linked to the worst of American Airlines Group, Inc., Delta Airlines Inc., Southwest Airlines Company, and United Continental Holdings, Inc." I spent close to an hour on the 23-page pricing supplement trying to understand what this investment was. It turned out to be a private placement security issued by BNP Paribas. The note pays out monthly at a 9% annual rate if none of the four airline stocks declines more than 50% from its price at the time the note was issued. When the note matures in three years, investors get their principal back if none of the stocks has a loss greater than 50%. If one or more of the stocks fall more than 50%, the principal amount returned is reduced by the percentage loss in the worst-performing stock. Finally, after the first six months, if all the stocks have increased in value from their price at the time the note was issued, the note is redeemed early and there are no further interest payments.

APPLYING THE INVESTMENT FRAMEWORK

Let's evaluate this note using the first five questions in our investing framework to decide if it is an investment worth pursuing.

The first question is, "What is it?" Typically, an investment with a 24-word name and a 23-page pricing supplement fails the "Can I explain it to someone else?" test. But let's dig deeper to see how it ranks on the other questions.

The second question is, "Is it investing, speculating, or gambling?" Does this autocallable contingent note have a positive expected return, indicating it is truly an investment? Is it a speculation where there is disagreement on whether the return will be positive or negative? Or is it a gamble with a negative expected return? There is no way to know for sure. The note is too complex and the returns too uncertain to even categorize. Another reason not to invest.

What is the upside? This is straightforward. The upside of the note is capped at 9% per year. The challenge is the note only generates income if none of the four airline stocks has declined more than 50%. If all four of the stocks increase in price, the note will be redeemed early, and the holder will no longer receive interest. Potentially, the holder would only receive two interest payments before the note is redeemed early. That would equate to a 4.5% return, which would be reduced by the 3.5% commission. That means the holder's return over the six-month period is 1%.

What is the downside? The maximum drawdown on the note is close to 100%, but that would require one of the airlines or the note issuer to go bankrupt. The risk of that is small but real. American Airlines Group's predecessor company AMR filed for bankruptcy in 2011, resulting in a near 100% loss for shareholders.[1]

What is the likelihood one of the airline stocks will fall by half while staying out of bankruptcy, resulting in a potential loss on the note of greater than 50%? There is a meaningful risk that will happen. All four airline stocks fell well over 50% during the global economic recession in

2008, with United Continental Holdings declining over 90%.[2] In addition, after exiting bankruptcy, the stock of American Airlines Group fell just over 50% from March 20, 2015, to June 24, 2016, and that was during an economic expansion.[3]

Our next question is, "Who is on the other side of the trade?" The first aspect of this question addresses counterparty risk. Since this is a private note, the counterparty is BNP Paribas. Payment on the note depends on the creditworthiness of BNP Paribas. Should the bank file for bankruptcy, the noteholders would line up with other unsecured creditors and likely lose all or most of their investment since there are no underlying assets backing the notes.

The second aspect of answering the question, "Who is on the other side of the trade?" is to consider this next question: "What does the seller BNP Paribas know about the future value and performance of these securities that the buyer doesn't?" A lot. No doubt BNP Paribas has modeled these notes extensively to ensure the bank earns a profit. The company certainly has an estimate of how likely it is an airline stock will fall 50% in price over the next three years. In fact, BNP Paribas probably hedged its risk to ensure it made a profit even if the bank ended up paying out 9% per year. It could be BNP Paribas had clients who were betting in a way opposite how these notes were structured. In that case, BNP Paribas would be indifferent to how airline stocks perform, because the bets of its clients and the note buyers would cancel each other out. BNP Paribas would earn a profit through the fee and commission income.

A return of 9% per year is attractive, and if I hadn't looked, I would have thought the likelihood of one of the airline stocks falling more than 50% in the next three years was small given it seems like such an extreme event. A buyer of this note is betting that airline stock prices won't fall by more than 50%. BNP Paribas doesn't bet when it sells these notes. It hedges to lock in a profit.

Our investment framework would have steered us away from buying the autocallable contingent income notes. The upside is capped at

9%, while there is a meaningful risk of capital loss. Unfortunately, that wasn't the case for the 97-year-old man. His broker sold him nine of these securities, earning 3.5% commission on each one. They made up 8% of his client's net worth. According to the Social Security Administration, a 97-year-old man has a life expectancy of 2.48 years and a 30% chance of dying in the next year.[4] In other words, these illiquid securities had longer expected lives than the client. The notes appear to be completely unsuitable for this man. Even if the notes had been simple to understand with a positive expected return, their illiquidity would seem to make them unsuitable given the short expected life span of the client. The broker should have recommended investments that could easily be sold if his client died, given his advanced age, unless perhaps the contingent payable notes were part of an estate plan. Three months after my listener told me about the autocallable notes, his father passed away, leaving these complicated investments for the estate's executor to figure out.

EVALUATING INVESTMENT VEHICLES

The liquidity, or the ability to exit an investment, is one component to consider in answering the sixth question in our investing framework, "What is the investment vehicle?" An investment vehicle is the instrument, product, or container that houses a particular investment strategy. The investment vehicle could be the actual instrument that generates the return such as an individual stock, bond, apartment building, or autocallable contingent income note. Or the vehicle could be an entity such as a mutual fund, closed-end fund, or ETF that has an investment advisor selecting the underlying stocks, bonds, or other securities. Sometimes there are several layers of investment vehicles such as a real estate investment trust ETF that invests in publicly traded real estate investment trusts that in turn own and collect rent on office buildings, apartments, and retail stores.

The expected return, the drivers of that return, and the risk as measured by volatility and maximum drawdown are attributes of investment vehicles. We have already covered those topics in earlier chapters. If an investment vehicle were a car, we already would have analyzed the engine, transmission, and brakes. Now we are turning to the other components such as the car's interior. Four additional attributes to consider when evaluating investment vehicles are liquidity, costs, structure, and pricing.

Liquidity

Liquidity measures how quickly and easily you can sell an investment, what is the cost for doing so, and how long after you sell do you receive your money. For example, stocks and ETFs have intraday liquidity because they can be sold throughout the market trading day on an exchange. Open-end mutual funds have end-of-day liquidity, as they trade after the market closes. Daily liquidity does not mean you get your money right away. In the United States, brokerage firms must make funds from the sale of publicly traded securities, such as stocks and ETFs, available to their clients within two business days.[5]

The liquidity provisions for private investments vary, and it is critical that we understand the terms before we invest. The autocallable contingent income note we analyzed has liquidity when it matures in three years. It also can be redeemed early on a quarterly basis after a six-month waiting period if all four airline stocks are selling at a price equal to or greater than their initial price when the note was issued.

The only reason to invest in a vehicle that doesn't have daily liquidity is if it has a higher expected return than its publicly traded counterpart, or it has some other attribute that justifies the illiquidity. Illiquidity premium is the term used to describe the additional return for investing in an illiquid asset. If a private investment is expected to have a higher expected return than a similar publicly traded security, then the next logical question is why. How is that higher return being generated?

For example, equity real estate investment trusts are securities that own commercial real estate properties such as office buildings, apartments, storage units, hotels, and retail locations such as strip malls. Most REITs are publicly traded with daily liquidity. There are also private REITs available on real estate crowdfunding platforms. The sponsors of these private REITs forecast they will generate a higher return than the public equity REIT market. The sponsors suggest they can achieve higher returns because they are able to purchase commercial real estate properties at attractive prices. Perhaps they can, but these platforms also compete against public REITs and other institutional investors to buy those same properties. A big reason that private REITs and private real estate funds are able to outperform the public REIT market is that private REITs and funds deploy more leverage. Nareit, a REIT research organization, reports that the average publicly traded equity REIT has 35 cents of debt for every dollar of assets it owns based on the assets' market value.[6] That compares with private real estate funds including private REITs that commonly have 50 to 85 cents of debt for every dollar of assets. If all goes well, higher debt levels result in higher returns for private real estate investors because each dollar of equity investors put into the deal can be leveraged to buy more income-generating assets. Higher debt balances are also more risky, because falling rents and property values can make it more difficult to service the debt, potentially leading to default and losses for the REIT investors.

In order to access the potentially higher return of private investments, investors must give up daily liquidity. For example, one crowdfunding platform allows investors to redeem their shares in private REITs on a quarterly basis. In the early years of the investment, there is a redemption fee of 2% to 3% to exit the investment. That redemption fee represents the cost of gaining liquidity for an illiquid investment. The manager also limits the amount of redemptions each quarter and reserves the right to not redeem any shares.[7]

Costs

Fees for investment vehicles can vary dramatically. Individual securities such as stocks and bonds have no fees other than the commission to exit and enter the investment, and some investing apps don't even charge commissions. Commingled vehicles such as mutual funds and ETFs typically have a management fee and other expenses that are paid to the advisor to select the underlying securities and operate the fund. Not all commingled vehicles have fees. Fidelity Investments offers several index mutual funds that have a zero expense ratio. Investment providers that offer products with no fees seek to make money in other ways such as offering additional fee-based services.

Private investments usually have higher expenses than public investments because there is less competition and the investment strategies tend to be more complex. The baseline annual management fees for some private investment vehicles can be 2% of assets or higher and can include incentive fees of 20% of the profits. The cost of an investment vehicle reduces the potential return, so as investors we have to decide if the cost is worth it. We explore investment costs in more depth in Chapter 8.

Structure

The structure of the investment vehicle reflects how it is organized. Is it publicly traded with daily liquidity, or is it a private investment that might not have liquidity for years? Is it a commingled vehicle such as a mutual fund with numerous investors owning the underlying shares, or is it structured as a separately managed account where the advisor is selecting individual securities for your account? Commingled vehicles usually have lower fees and lower account minimums than separately managed accounts, but they also give investors less control in terms of recognizing losses and gains for tax purposes. An unwary investor might purchase new shares in a mutual fund later in the year, and then be surprised when the mutual fund makes a large capital gains distribution in December that is taxable to the investor even though the investor didn't participate in the gains. Further, those gains might have been caused by other investors exiting the fund, thereby forcing the manager to sell securities to meet those redemptions. In other words, actions by other investors can result in additional costs to all investors in a commingled fund. Still, most individuals and many institutions invest via commingled funds such as ETFs and mutual funds because they provide more options, they have daily liquidity, and the overall expenses are lower.

Investment vehicles have offering documents that describe the structure, terms, and other characteristics of the investment. A publicly traded investment will have a prospectus, while a private investment will have an offering memorandum. Investors should review these documents before undertaking a new investment. These documents are the best source to answer the question, "What is it?"

Pricing

A final attribute to consider when evaluating an investment vehicle is how its price is determined and whether that price equals what the investment is worth. The prices of some investments such as stocks are determined by investors as they buy and sell shares in a secondary market such as on a stock exchange. The prices for other investments such as bonds are set by dealers as they assess what the demand is and what similar securities are selling for. Finally, the prices of some investments, such as open-end mutual funds, are determined by the investment sponsor based on the value of the underlying assets held by the funds.

The price of an investment does not always reflect its value. As we discussed in earlier chapters, the present value of an investment is the price in today's dollar of its future income stream, such as dividends or interest. Because there can be uncertainty regarding that future income stream, an investor is not always certain the price equals the intrinsic value. Yet there is an aspect of price and value when it comes to investment vehicles that goes beyond the theoretical value. There are times when the price of an investment vehicle does not equal the value of its underlying holdings as reflected in their individual prices. The investment vehicle might be priced at \$100 per share, but the value of what the vehicle owns might be worth \$110 per share. That means the vehicle is selling at a 10% discount to the value of its underlying holdings.

The value of a commingled investment vehicle such as a mutual fund, ETF, or closed-end fund is known as its net asset value (NAV). It is calculated by taking the value of a fund's assets including cash, subtracting any liabilities, and dividing by the number of shares outstanding. Open-end mutual fund sponsors calculate the net asset value at the end of each trading day and set the market price per share equal to the NAV. That means shareholders that exit or enter the fund do so at a market price that always equals the per share value of the underlying holdings (i.e., the NAV). Open-end mutual funds facilitate purchases and redemptions by creating or eliminating shares. The number of shares outstanding is tied to demand from underlying investors. There is potentially an unlimited amount of shares. This is why mutual funds that operate in this way are called open-end mutual funds.

CLOSED-END FUNDS

Closed-end funds like open-end mutual funds are commingled funds overseen by professional managers who select stocks, bonds, and other securities. Where closed-end funds differ from open-end mutual funds is closed-end funds have a fixed number of shares. The shares are created through an initial public offering (IPO) that raises capital from investors. The closed-end fund manager then invests that capital using the strategy outlined in the fund's prospectus. After the IPO, investors that want to enter or exit the fund do so by buying or selling shares in the secondary market on a stock exchange. Because the price of a closed-end fund is determined by investors trading the fixed number of shares in the secondary market, rather than the fund sponsor, the share price frequently doesn't equal the net asset value. Closed-end funds typically sell at a premium or discount to the net asset value. For example, in October 2018, the average discount across all closed-end funds in the United States was 6.73%.[8] There were also a handful of closed-end funds selling for premiums of greater than 25%, with at least one fund selling at a greater than 50% premium.[9] It makes little economic sense to buy a closed-end fund that is selling for 50% more per share than what its underlying holdings are worth. Yet the premiums persist.

At $275 billion, the total value of all closed-end funds in the United States is small compared with the $18.7 trillion invested in mutual funds and $3.4 trillion in ETFs.[10] Closed-end funds have much higher fees than mutual funds and ETFs, and most employ leverage in order to increase their yields. In addition, most investors in closed-end funds are individuals. That means when you buy or sell a closed-end fund, it is usually an individual on the other side of the trade. Given that closed-end funds trade on an exchange, are owned primarily by individuals, and deploy leverage, they are significantly more volatile than open-end mutual funds even if they own similar security types.

During periods of market turmoil, closed-end fund discounts tend to widen as individual investors dump their holdings. Purchasing a closed-end bond fund that is selling at a significantly wider discount than its historical average can be an attractive investment, as you are able to collect interest income while waiting for the discount to narrow. That is why I think trading closed-end funds is a more compelling strategy than trading foreign exchange and commodities. With closed-end funds, you are not competing against institutions or algorithms, but against other individual investors. Most closed-end funds have a positive expected return because of the income stream, which means it is not a zero-sum game as it is with forex or commodity futures where there is a winner for every loser. Of course, investors in closed-end funds need to be aware of the much higher costs and the leverage, which can magnify losses in down markets.

EXCHANGE-TRADED FUNDS

Exchange-traded funds are marketable securities that seek to track a specific index or segment of the capital markets, such as large-company stocks, bonds, or REITs. Most ETFs track passive benchmarks, such as the S&P 500 Index for U.S. large-company stocks or the Russell 2000 Index for U.S. small-company stocks. Prior to the introduction of the first ETF in 1993, investors that wanted to passively invest in specific segments of the market were limited to index mutual funds. ETFs are similar to open-end mutual funds in that there is no limit to the number of shares outstanding, but unlike mutual funds, ETFs trade throughout the day on an exchange in the same way closed-end funds do.

ETFs are unique among commingled funds in how new shares are created. Recall that an open-end mutual fund sponsor creates or redeems shares at the end of the trading day based on that day's buy and sell orders. ETF sponsors create and redeem shares throughout the trading day as well as at the end of the day, working closely with large institutional investment and financial firms called authorized participants. Examples of authorized participants include JP Morgan, Goldman Sachs, Citigroup, and Morgan Stanley.[11] Each day the ETF sponsor publishes a list of securities and their weights called the creation basket that is representative of the securities held by the ETF. New ETF shares are created when the ETF sponsor transfers ETF shares to an authorized participant in exchange for a basket of securities that approximates the creation basket. Similarly, ETF shares are redeemed when the ETF sponsor exchanges the securities that compose the creation basket for shares of the ETF held by the authorized participant. These newly issued and redeemed ETF shares are called creation units, and they typically consist of trading blocks ranging from 25,000 to 250,000 ETF shares.

These in-kind transfers between authorized participants and ETF sponsors during and at the end of the trading day help keep the price of the ETF in line with its net asset value. Throughout the trading day the

ETF sponsor publishes the net asset value every 15 to 60 seconds. If there is a discrepancy between the ETF's NAV and its price, institutional investors can earn essentially a risk-free profit by buying or short selling the ETF while at the same time buying or short selling the underlying securities that make up the creation basket designated by the ETF. Short selling is an investment technique that involves selling investment securities borrowed from another investor. If the investment security falls in price, investors make a profit when they close out the short position because they buy back the investment security to return to the original owner at a lower price than what they sold the borrowed shares for.

For example, suppose the ETF was selling in the open market for $50 per share but the net asset value was $55. The authorized participant could buy ETF shares for $50 in the open market and exchange them with the ETF sponsors for the creation basket securities, which are worth $55 per share. The securities received in kind could then be sold in the open market, locking in a $5 per share profit for the authorized participant. Within a very short time, demand in the open market to buy the ETF to lock in the risk-free profit would push up the ETF price to $55, in line with the NAV.

Conversely, if the ETF was selling for $55 and the NAV was $50, the authorized participant could short sell the ETF by borrowing shares and selling them for $55 each. At the same time, the authorized participant could buy the creation basket securities that are worth $50 per share, exchange the basket with the ETF sponsor for new ETF shares, and close out the short position by returning these newly issued ETF shares to the account from which the original ETF shares were borrowed. This would lock in a $5 per share profit, because the authorized participant sold borrowed ETF shares for $55 each in the open market, but it only cost $50 each to get new ETF shares from the ETF sponsor to close out the short position. Again, within a short period of time, there would be sufficient selling of the ETF by authorized participants seeking to lock in this risk-free profit that the ETF price would fall to $50 per share.

Flash Crashes and Other ETF Risks

While the significant growth in ETFs has given investors access to many different asset types at a very low cost, that convenience has not come without risk. Academic studies show that the growth in ETFs has increased the volatility of both the indices that ETFs track and the underlying securities that ETFs own.[12] Much of this increased volatility is due to the trading by authorized participants seeking to profit from price discrepancies between ETF prices and NAVs. According to a paper published by S&P, this increased trading activity "may consume liquidity from securities and cause prices to drift from levels supported by fundamentals when consumption is large relative to the liquidity available."[13] In other words, there is a potential price impact if security prices drift further from their intrinsic value as more and more trading activity is linked to keeping passive ETF prices in sync with their underlying holdings rather than trading activity by investors with a fundamental view of a security's intrinsic value.

Market makers and authorized participants need timely price information and the ability to trade ETFs and their underlying securities in order to facilitate a smoothly functioning ETF market. During periods of market turmoil and high volatility, liquidity can dry up, leading to severe price gaps and trading halts in some securities, including ETFs, if their prices move outside a specified price band.[14] Without the ability to get accurate security prices due to trading halts, the ETFs' pricing mechanism breaks down as authorized participants pull back, leading to severe price dislocations.

This type of "flash crash" occurred on August 24, 2015. It is an example of a market avalanche that is characteristic of complex adaptive systems. Recall that a complex adaptive system consists of a wide variety of interconnected inputs and agents that adapt and learn over time. As the system evolves, complex interactions can lead to unexpected outcomes. On that day in August 2015, global stock markets were already down 3% to 5% before the U.S. market opened, leading to a spike in the volume of sell orders to be executed at market prices when the U.S. market opened. The New York Stock Exchange reported the volume of market orders was four times greater than average that morning. By 9:40 a.m., nearly half of the securities on the New York Stock Exchange had yet to begin normal trading due to stock-specific trading halts, known as limit up–limit down rules.[15] Trading halts on individual stocks and ETFs based on short-term price movements were implemented after the flash crash of May 6, 2010, in which many stocks and ETFs plummeted more than 50% and then rebounded over a period of approximately 36 minutes.[16]

Individual trading halts on over 1,300 securities prevented authorized participants from engaging in the normal trading activity that keeps ETF prices in line with net asset values.[17] As a result, there were significant price discrepancies, with some ETFs falling over 20% while the indices they tracked were down approximately 5%. There were also significant price discrepancies for ETFs that track the same index.[18] These price differences meant some ETF investors that had market orders to sell ETF shares had their trades executed at prices significantly below what they expected and far below the price the ETF was trading at later in the day.[19]

The significant increase in algorithmic high-frequency trading could lead to more severe flash crashes in the future. Charles Himmelberg, co-chief markets economist at Goldman Sachs, wrote in a note to clients that "when shocks of unknown origin cause sudden price declines, HFTs [high frequency traders] may have reason to assume that the shock is being driven by fundamental news (e.g., if the price decline follows a complex macro surprise or dramatic policy announcement). Under these circumstances, HFTs are at higher risk of being adversely selected by more fundamentally informed traders, so their optimal response is to withdraw liquidity by widening their quotes or by withdrawing them altogether."[20] This lack of liquidity could lead to price drops that set off trading halts in some securities, disrupting the trading activity of ETF-authorized participants. A negative feedback loop could then ensue, with high-frequency traders withdrawing even more liquidity as they refuse to trade, leading to even greater price drops, more trading halts, and price dislocations between ETFs and the underlying indices they track.[21]

How to Protect Yourself When Implementing Trades

While ETFs appear straightforward and easy to use, there is a great deal of complexity lurking beneath the surface. One of our responsibilities as portfolio managers is to make sure we get the best price when initiating trades for our accounts. When we buy or sell ETFs or other securities that trade on an exchange including closed-end funds, we should never place market orders in which the security is bought or sold at the prevailing market price. Markets can move quickly, so the market order could be filled at a vastly different price from what was displayed on the computer screen at the time the order was placed. Instead, we should specify the price at which we are willing to buy or sell the security. This is called a limit order. In most cases, the price we specify should be somewhere between the bid and ask price. The bid price is the current offer if you want to sell shares, while the ask price is the current offer if you want to buy shares. In a normal market environment, the trade should be executed at the designated limit price, but if for some reason there is another flash crash, by using limit orders we are protected against getting our buy or sell orders filled at undesirable prices.

To date, ETF-related flash crashes have been isolated, and the price discrepancies have been resolved within a few hours, not causing financial harm to long-term ETF holders. I continue to own ETFs in my personal portfolio. Still, I will monitor how the market develops to make sure flash crashes don't become more frequent and risks become more elevated.

As portfolio managers, we should also study the prospectus or offering memorandum of any investment vehicle we are considering, paying particular attention to the fees and liquidity provisions, which can vary significantly from one investment to another.

CHAPTER SUMMARY

- An investment vehicle is an instrument, product, or container that houses a particular investment strategy. Examples of investment vehicles include individual stocks, bonds, REITs, ETFs, and mutual funds.

- Investment vehicle attributes include the expected return, risk as measured by the potential maximum drawdown, liquidity, costs, structure, and pricing.

- Open-end mutual funds, closed-end funds, and ETFs are investment vehicles with daily liquidity. ETFs and open-end mutual funds have no cap on the number of shares outstanding, while closed-end funds have a fixed number of shares.

- ETF and closed-end fund prices are determined by investors as they trade shares in the secondary market. Closed-end fund prices can differ significantly from the net asset value. ETFs have an in-kind transfer mechanism to create and redeem shares that keeps the price in line with the net asset value during normal market environments.

- On rare occasions, such as during flash crashes, the pricing mechanism for ETFs has broken down, resulting in severe price differences between ETFs, the value of the underlying holdings, and the index they seek to track.

- We can ensure the best price when trading ETFs and other securities by using limit orders.

7

What Does It Take to Be Successful?

Identifying What Drives Investment Outcomes

THE TEN QUESTIONS

1. What is it?
2. Is it investing, speculating, or gambling?
3. What is the upside?
4. What is the downside?
5. Who is on the other side of the trade?
6. What is the investment vehicle?
7. **What does it take to be successful?**
8. Who is getting a cut?
9. How does it impact your portfolio?
10. Should you invest?

QUESTION SEVEN: WHAT DOES IT TAKE TO BE SUCCESSFUL?

All investments have return drivers, such as income, cash flow growth, leverage, and other attributes that determine their performance. Successful portfolios have a diversified mix of dependable return drivers that we have identified beforehand.

In Chapter 4, I shared how mentors of former Federal Reserve chairman Ben Bernanke told him, "If you never miss a plane, you're spending too much time in airports."[1] Missing a flight can be quite disruptive to our travel plans, which is why we try to arrive at the airport early (but not too early). I have missed my share of flights, but there is one missed flight that stands out because of why I missed it. I got lost on the way to the airport.

When I lived in Cincinnati and worked as an investment advisor, the airfares were notoriously pricey because the Cincinnati/Northern Kentucky International Airport was a major Delta Airlines hub at the time. Consequently, I would on occasion park my car at the Cincinnati airport, pick up a one-way rental vehicle, drive to the airport in Lexington, Kentucky, take a flight back to Cincinnati, and then continue on to my final destination. On my return, I would get off the plane in Cincinnati and drive home. This ridiculous itinerary would often save $600 or more on my airfare, particularly on flights to New Orleans where I had several advisory clients.

The Lexington airport is not situated by a major interstate highway. It is west of the city along a somewhat rural route. On one of my trips to Lexington, I decided to leave Interstate 75 that connects Cincinnati to Lexington and take a shortcut to the airport. This was before mobile phones had map applications, and I didn't have a GPS unit in my rental car. Nor did I have a map. All I had was a general sense of where the Lexington airport should be, given my previous visits.

I drove among the bluegrass hills where horses pastured behind rail fences. My route would often dead-end as I traversed the bucolic terrain, requiring me to choose to go left or right. After 30 minutes of driving, it became clear I was lost. It was a cloudy day so I couldn't get my bearings from the sun. I just kept driving, hoping I would see the air traffic control tower or run into a major highway. After 45 minutes, I began to panic, as the boarding time for my plane was fast approaching and I was still hopelessly lost. Another 30 minutes passed before I finally found the airport, but by then it was too late. I missed my flight and had to call my client to explain that I needed to cancel our dinner plans as I had experienced a "travel delay."

Although I was lost, I wasn't completely lost. I knew I was in Kentucky in the general vicinity of the airport, even though I didn't know exactly where I was. Daniel Boone said, "I was never lost in the woods in my whole life, though once I was confused for three days."[2] That was me. Not completely lost. Just confused.

In this book's Introduction I shared a quote from former professional poker player Annie Duke, who wrote: "What makes a decision great is not that it has a great outcome. A great decision is the result of a good process. . . ."[3] Missing a flight is a bad outcome. Sometimes that outcome is beyond our control, such as our arriving flight is late, and we miss our connection. Missing a flight because we get lost on the way to the airport is the result of a bad process. As investors, we can't dictate portfolio outcomes, but we can increase the odds of favorable investment returns by having good processes. That's where the ten-question framework described in this book can help. Answering a series of questions before we invest is a process that can help us weed out inappropriate investments. That process can also help us identify attractive investment opportunities. The seventh question in the framework, "What does it take to be successful?" allows us to be very clear about what drives favorable investment outcomes. While we can't control whether an investment achieves a positive return, we can understand what must happen for the investment to be a success. For example, we know that investments that generate income in the form of interest, dividends, or rent are more likely to have a positive return than investments that don't.

On another occasion, also due to a bad process, my Uber driver got lost on the way to my Airbnb rental in Brooklyn, even though he had a map. An app on the Uber driver's phone gave him step-by-step directions of how to get to the apartment. But he wasn't patient enough to follow the directions. He would get frustrated when stuck in traffic and not wait for the designated turn. He would turn early and not necessarily toward our destination. At that point, the app would reroute him to the new, quickest way to the apartment. There were several problems with the driver's methods. First, he actually had no idea where he was. He was entirely dependent on the app to tell him where to go next. Second, the app wouldn't let him zoom out in order to get a broader perspective of our location. When he made an early turn, he had no idea if he was turning toward or away from the apartment. Third, the driver spoke very little English, so whenever I tried to help out, he became even more frustrated. We went in circles for about 25 minutes until we found ourselves in traffic on Interstate 278 in Brooklyn Heights where it was no longer easy to get off the highway. We then just went with the traffic flow. At that point, the driver settled down and stopped trying to second-guess the app, and we made it to the apartment.

In investing, there are no step-by-step instructions that can guarantee a successful outcome. Instead, we have rules of thumb that give us a sense of whether we are heading in the right direction. Those rules of thumb allow us to zoom out to get a broader view as we categorize various investment opportunities with regard to their potential return, risk, and return drivers. Return drivers are an investment's attributes that determine its performance. This form of navigation is known as wayfinding. We get in trouble as investors when we forget we are wayfinders and believe outcomes are certain.

WAYFINDING

The American explorers Lewis and Clark were wayfinders. They didn't have a detailed map as they explored the western United States looking for the easiest route to the Pacific Ocean. Instead, they had wayfinding tools such as a compass, a chronometer to calculate longitude, and the book *A Practical Introduction to Spherics and Nautical Astronomy.* These wayfinding tools helped them generally head in the right direction. Lewis and Clark spent $2,324 on equipment for their expedition including boats, oars, camping supplies, clothing, medicine, and armaments. They also bought presents for Native Americans, including 4,600 sewing needles, 130 rolls of tobacco, 288 knives, 288 brass thimbles, 144 small scissors, and 25 pounds of colored beads.[4] When you are wayfinding, you need to be prepared for the unexpected.

Early twentieth-century British philosopher and logician Carveth Read shared what could be considered the wayfinder's motto, "It is better to be vaguely right, than precisely wrong."[5] The seventh question in our framework helps us distinguish whether our investment success depends on being vaguely right or precisely right. If our investment success depends on being precisely right, then even if we are a *little* wrong, we will be unsuccessful and potentially lose money.

We have already explored investment examples that require us to be precisely right to generate a profit. These include foreign currency, commodity futures, and binary options. These are zero-sum games in which for every winner there is a loser. They often require us to outsmart other investors. Speculations as a rule require us to be precisely right about the future. We will only gain a profit with gold, art, or cryptocurrencies if investors are willing to pay more in the future for these non-income-producing assets. Investments that generate income have a second return driver apart from price appreciation. The price of an income-generating asset might fall if investors choose to pay less for the income stream, but an investor could still achieve a positive return because the investment generated enough interest or dividends to offset the price decline.

Not all speculations are inappropriate if they are a small percentage of an individual's net worth. For example, my wife, LaPriel, and I own some antique furniture that may or may not go up in value. If the pieces fall in price, that is okay, because in the meantime we get a lot of use and enjoyment from the furniture. I also speculate in gold coins. Gold has been around for millennia and can be used as an inflation hedge. Over the long term, its price has appreciated more than inflation, but not every year. Gold can lag inflation over extended periods because its price appreciates only if speculators are willing to pay more. I believe gold will go up in the future, but I also know that my gold allocation is a specific bet that requires me to be precisely right to make a profit. Because I might be wrong, I make sure my allocation to gold is small enough that the personal financial harm caused by the loss will not negatively impact my lifestyle. Recall that the downside of an investment is a function of not just its potential loss, but the personal harm caused by the loss.

RETURN DRIVERS

As we discussed earlier, three drivers determine the return for most investments (as opposed to speculations):

1. **CASH FLOW.** The income from interest, dividends, or rents that is distributed to the asset owner
2. **CASH FLOW GROWTH.** How the income stream or cash flow grows over time
3. **CHANGE IN VALUATION.** What investors are willing to pay for the income stream now versus later

These return drivers explain why investments have positive expected returns. The simplest way to harvest those returns is through the use of index mutual funds or ETFs. These passive investment vehicles allow us to purchase baskets of individual securities without having to worry whether a specific underlying holding is priced correctly in that its market price equals its intrinsic value. Recall that intrinsic value, also known as the present value, is the price in today's dollar of an investment's future income stream, such as dividends or interest.

An alternative to buying index funds or passive ETFs is to seek to identify securities where the market price is less than its intrinsic value. This adds another layer of complexity to successful investing, as we are no longer just harvesting the returns of the overall market. Instead, we are seeking to earn excess returns through security selection because we believe that the market price is wrong, that the consensus of investors is incorrect. Howard Marks, author and co-chairman of Oaktree Capital, wrote: "All investors who follow a given asset have (or should have) opinions regarding its intrinsic value. The market price of the asset reflects the consensus of those opinions, meaning investors collectively have set the price. That's where buyers and sellers agree to transact. The buyers buy because they think it's a smart investment at the current price, and the sellers sell because they think it's fully priced or overpriced there."[6]

There is no doubt prices of individual securities are not always correct. The price of a security does not always reflect its intrinsic value. The question is do we have the skill to identify those mispriced securities? Are we smarter than other investors? Most professional investors fail to outperform the market, but some do, as do some individuals. But harvesting those excess returns requires us to be precisely right in order to be successful.

Andrea, a listener to my podcast, wrote me:

One thing I've heard you say on the podcast and many other times, is "the only reason to buy an individual stock is if you believe that the market is wrong." I'm wondering if you really think that? I'm asking this because I can think of lots of reasons to buy individual stocks, such as having control of taxable events, finding and investing in a product/company that I really like a lot, avoiding mutual fund/ETF expenses, wanting to have a good dividend that you can't normally find in an ETF or mutual fund, and then sometimes just wanting to have a little "mad money" to play around with.[7]

I agree with Andrea that it is fun to play around by buying individual stocks, but is the only reason to invest in an individual stock because you believe the market is wrong? It turns out it is not the only reason. Just the main and most important one.

I initially replied to Andrea that I really believed that. An incorrect price was the only reason to purchase an individual stock. Later, in my e-mail newsletter that week, I shared how a hair stylist I sometimes visit when I am in New York City likes to buy individual stocks. I gave him my spiel that the only reason to buy an individual stock is if the market consensus about the company's prospects is wrong. He disagreed, but then went on to make a strong case for why he felt Apple's stock was undervalued, including mentioning that Warren Buffet owns it. By definition, though, if a company is undervalued, then its current price is wrong.

My stylist is approaching this the right way. He has analyzed Apple and believes investors are underestimating the company's staying power and its earnings growth potential. A company's stock price should reflect the present value or price in today's dollars of its future dividends, which are a function of its future earnings. If earnings and dividends are going to be higher than what the consensus of investors believes, then the company's intrinsic value per share is higher than its current price. That's another way of saying the market is wrong and the stock is undervalued.

Some Stocks Are Too Expensive

I believe there are many stocks that are mispriced, including many that are too expensive. Rob Arnott and his colleagues pointed out some examples of stocks that were too pricey.

At the beginning of 2000, the 10 largest market-cap tech stocks in the United States, collectively representing a 25% share of the S&P 500 Index—Microsoft, Cisco, Intel, IBM, AOL, Oracle, Dell, Sun, Qualcomm, and HP—did not live up to the excessively optimistic expectations. Over the next 18 years, *not a single one beat the market*: five produced positive returns, averaging 3.2% a year compounded, far lower than the market return, and two failed outright. Of the five that produced negative returns, the average outcome was a loss of 7.2% a year, or 12.6% a year less than the S&P 500.[8]

These stocks underperformed because the consensus of investors had assumed earnings growth rates that were too high. The companies disappointed, so the share prices either fell or didn't appreciate as much as the overall stock market.

Some Stocks Are Too Cheap

Other stocks are mispriced because they are too cheap. They are undervalued. The consensus of investor opinion can be wrong such that the price of an individual stock doesn't reflect its intrinsic value because investors are too pessimistic. When investors are too pessimistic and a company surprises to the upside, then collectively investors are willing to transact at a higher price for the stock. The price jumps, often outperforming the overall market. When investors are too optimistic and a company surprises to the downside, then, collectively, investors are willing to transact at a lower price. The price drops. Every day, stock prices react to a constant stream of surprises and changing investor narratives, the stories investors tell themselves. Over time, these positive and negative surprises that impact individual stocks cancel each other, so that the overall stock market performance is primarily driven by the dividend yield and the growth of that dividend over time. Yet at the same time, the overall valuation of the market can shift as investors in aggregate are willing to pay more or less for those earnings and dividend streams. Asset classes become cheaper or more expensive relative to their historical averages.

After reading my newsletter, Andrea replied:

I think your wording is throwing me off. I've bought individual stocks thinking that the stock is both fairly valued by the market AND that it will outperform the market. Here's an example: A couple of years ago I needed to buy about twenty Christmas gifts for adults and children I was working with, and I didn't want to spend a fortune. I went to the mall and saw a new store I had never seen before called Five Below. I was able to find all my gifts plus a few more things I couldn't resist. I was so amazed that I came home and researched the company. It turned out that they were a fairly new company, no debt, every item $5 and below, and they were/are expanding geographically across the country from east to west. The financials looked good. I bought. I absolutely did not think that the market had anything wrong at the price I bought at. But I did think that if things continued to go well, and other people liked their store as much as I did, that it could outperform the market. It was a gamble. For one thing there's this competitor called Amazon. But a lot of people need to buy last minute gifts for their kid's birthday parties, and other random events, and can't wait for an Amazon shipment. Turns out I was thinking correctly, but does that mean the market was wrong at the time I bought?[9]

I replied that I indeed believed the market price was wrong at the time she purchased. I reiterated that the theoretical or correct price of the stock is the present value (or value in today's dollars) of its future dividends (which are in turn based on its future earnings). So the stock price should already reflect that things will go well and more and more people will shop at the store. There was already a growth assumption priced into the stock. For it to outperform, the stock needed to grow its earnings faster than what other investors were already assuming based on the price-to-earnings ratio that was reflected in the price. It needed to surprise to the upside. If the company had missed earnings estimates, it would have surprised to the downside and lagged the market just as the ten largest U.S. stocks at the peak of the dot-com bubble underperformed the market over the subsequent 18 years.

Andrea pushed back. She wrote: "I do understand present value, growth assumptions, etc. in the pricing of stocks. But I am still having a real problem with the word 'only.'"[10] She then shared two examples of stocks she purchased and why: "In 2013 I bought Raytheon, the defense contractor, because I wanted to hedge my portfolio in case of a war or conflict such as that. Since there was no conflict on the horizon, should the market have priced that in anyway?" She pointed out that Raytheon stock jumped after the U.S. initiated missile strikes against Syria in 2018, something that couldn't be known when she bought the stock in 2013.

She continued:

> In 2016, I bought the bakery Flowers Food for the dividend, inflation protection with a product that can reprice quickly if prices start going up, and protection against economic downturn with a staple that people will buy no matter what. This stock was up on the days the market crashed last week, so I believe the purpose I purchased it for is valid. Also, this stock was purchased as an alternative to bonds/fixed income, which were paying next to nothing at the time. I have no intention of selling it even though I don't expect this stock to outperform the market.[11]

There she had me. She bought individual stocks not because she thought the market price was wrong, but to hedge or protect her portfolio against unforeseen macro or political events. She anticipated investor demand for those stocks would change if certain events occurred. Protecting your portfolio from unforeseeable events could be a valid reason to purchase an individual stock, although it is still a concentrated bet that may not perform as expected. I prefer to get protection from unseen events by holding multiple asset classes with different return drivers rather than relying on individual stocks. Andrea acts as a portfolio and risk manager. She allocates her investment capital to different assets including individual stocks that she believes will behave differently under different economic and market conditions. She has a diversified mix of return drivers so that all her investments don't fall in price at the same time, causing undue financial harm.

DIVIDEND INVESTING

Returning to our three return drivers, why don't we just buy high-income-generating investments where the cash flow is growing quickly and which sell for low prices? Unfortunately, in today's hyperconnected world, rarely do all three criteria match up. High-dividend stocks tend to have lower dividend and earnings growth rates than low-dividend-paying stocks, because low-dividend-paying stocks or stocks that pay no dividend at all can reinvest more of their earnings in high-growth opportunities. Likewise, the stocks of high earnings growth companies are usually more expensive than the stocks of companies whose earnings are growing more slowly.

Professionals at Ned Davis Research conduct an ongoing study in which they separate the U.S. stock market into dividend-paying stocks and non-dividend-paying stocks. They further separate the dividend-paying stocks into one of three categories based on the company's dividend policy over the previous 12 months. Has the company increased its dividend, kept it the same, or cut the dividend? Going back to 1972 and over most intermediate periods in between, dividend-paying stocks performed better than both non-dividend-paying stocks and the U.S. stock market overall as measured by the equal-weighted S&P 500 Index, where each stock has an equal-size weight.[12]

In the study, non-dividend-paying stocks lagged the overall stock market. That suggests that while companies that don't pay dividends might grow their earnings faster than dividend-paying companies, investors who pay high multiples for these stocks as measured by the price-to-earnings ratio are often disappointed when the companies fail to match the lofty growth expectations priced into the stocks. The result is these high-flying stocks often drop in price and lag the overall market, as previously enthusiastic investors are unwilling to pay as high a multiple of earnings for them. The best-performing category in the Ned Davis Research study consisted of companies that initiated or increased their dividends, while the worst-performing category consisted of companies that cut or eliminated their dividends.[13]

Ned Davis Research adjusts the constituents and rebalances the sub-indices on a monthly basis, which would make this dividend strategy difficult to implement in a live portfolio due to trading costs. There are, however, exchange-traded funds that seek to replicate the performance of indices that focus on companies that consistently grow their dividends. For example, the S&P 500 High Yield Dividend Aristocrats Index is an index comprising just over 100 companies that have increased their dividend every year for 20 years. The index has outperformed the broad U.S. stock market as measured by the S&P 1500 Index over the long term, but there have been extended periods when it has underperformed.[14] Like most investment strategies, dividend investing goes in and out of favor. During times when investors favor stocks with consistent dividend growth, they are willing to pay more for them, which pushes up their valuation and lowers their dividend yield. That can lead to lower returns in the future relative to a more diversified indexing strategy that contains both dividend-paying and non-dividend-paying stocks.

Factor Investing and Smart Beta

Dividend investing is an investment strategy that seeks to outperform the overall stock market because of the higher income. That higher income is known as a factor, a broad, persistent driver of return. Economic growth and inflation are examples of macro factors that have an impact on asset class performance. There are also tradable factors. These are persistent return drivers that can generate a performance premium relative to the overall market. That performance premium is harvested not through trying to identify individual mispriced securities, but by investing in a basket of securities with similar characteristics. For example, value is a factor that has generated outperformance relative to the overall stock market over long periods of time. Value works because investors are overly pessimistic about the growth prospects of companies suffering through bad times and overly optimistic about high-growth companies. This leads to value stocks getting too cheap and surprising to the upside, while growth stocks get too expensive and disappoint. Of course, value investing can also go through long periods of underperformance relative to the overall stock market, so in some sense the value premium is compensation to investors for having to suffer through bad times.[15]

Smart beta is a term used for investment strategies that systematically seek to harvest the return premium from tradable factors. Besides value, other smart beta strategies include investing in high-quality stocks, low-volatility stocks, or stocks experiencing strong price momentum. One challenge with smart beta strategies is it can be difficult to separate the excess return arising from the actual factor from the excess return due to the smart beta strategy becoming more popular and thus more expensive. If the outperformance relative to the stock market is because the smart beta strategy has become more expensive, then that could mean the smart beta strategy could underperform in the future.[16] In addition, the potential excess return from smart beta strategies can also be diluted by trading costs, taxes, and manager fees.[17]

MARKET CONDITIONS

In order to fully answer the question, "What does it take to be successful?" it is important to understand not only the drivers of the underlying asset class such as the yield, cash flow growth, and change in cash flow multiple, but the current conditions. Howard Marks wrote: "As difficult as it is to know the future, it's really not that hard to understand the present. What we need to do is 'take the market's temperature.' If we are alert and perceptive, we can gauge the behavior of those around us and from that judge what we should do."[18]

For example, several years ago I invested in a student housing project that a friend was developing. Unfortunately, this friend passed away before the project was completed. A new developer agreed to take over the project, and during a conference call the developer and his staff presented the assumptions they used for their financial modeling. When investing in real estate, a key metric is the capitalization rate, also known as the cap rate. The cap rate is calculated by dividing the project's annual net operating income by the project's cost or value. Net operating income is the income a project earns after deducting operating expenses such as taxes, property management fees, etc. At the time, the prevailing cap rate for similar projects in this college town was 5.75%. The developer's baseline assumption was a cap rate of 6.25%, and he and his staff presented a sensitivity analysis based on varying rents, occupancy rates, and cap rates. The cap rate in their analysis ranged from 5.75% to 6.75%.

A worst-case scenario of 6.75% seemed low to me, seeing that student housing cap rates reached 7.75% in 2009 and were over 8% in 2003.[19] When I asked the developer what would happen if cap rates rose to 8%, he felt that was an unrealistic assumption, but he admitted that if cap rates reached that level, the project would lose money if it were sold. The reason it would lose money if sold is unless rents increase, the only way a real estate project's cap rate can rise is if the value of the property falls. At an 8% cap rate, this student housing project would fall below the cost of building it.

At this time, strong demand by institutional investors to own these cash flow–generating assets in stable college towns had pushed up valuations and lowered the yield. The market was pricey, and an increase in interest rates could cause capitalization rates to spike and property values to fall. Despite the risk of rising cap rates, I went ahead and stayed in the project since my investment was relatively small, and I wanted to see how it worked out. That turned out to be a good decision, as the new developer was able to build the project and fully lease the units.

The unfortunate passing of my friend was also a sobering reminder that some investments are highly reliant on the skill of certain individuals to be successful. If those individuals are no longer around, because they either leave for another job, get sick, or pass away, the investment could be at risk. As an investment advisor, when I researched money managers, I would always ask about transition plans in case the key principals "got hit by a bus." Private real estate development is dependent on the efforts of specific individuals, perhaps even ourselves if we purchase a rental property. I had lunch with this friend just a few months before he was diagnosed with a brain tumor. He felt great and was excited to give me an update on the student housing project. Eight weeks after the cancer diagnosis, he passed away. Unfortunately, there was not a clear transition plan outlined in the operating agreement in case he died. While I didn't expect my friend to pass, one reason I kept my investment small was I knew he was working alone, so a successful outcome depended on his individual effort.

A private investment, such as a local real estate project, where success is dependent on our own or another's work, can be a good diversifier because the return drivers are not tied to public markets. Several years ago, LaPriel and I bought a single-family home in this same college town and worked with a contractor to convert it into a triplex that could be rented to students. Enrollment was growing at the local college, and we bought the property at an attractive price. Consequently, the success was dependent less on being sensitive to market dynamics and more on working through the permitting process and making sure the remodel came in on budget. Our original intent was to keep the triplex as a rental, but I couldn't find a suitable property management company. After spending part of New Year's Eve trying to fix the water heater, I realized I didn't like managing rental properties, so we sold the building at a profit and got out of the rental real estate business.

In this particular transaction, we didn't use leverage by borrowing money to buy the building or pay for the remodel. Leverage can be used to enhance the return of real estate projects or other investments, but the investment should be able to generate an attractive return without leverage. Investments that require leverage to succeed are significantly more risky because there is less of a margin of safety to protect the investor in case things go wrong.

Another example of a return driver that isn't dependent on the public market is distressed debt managers who buy the debt of companies that are in or near bankruptcy. These distressed debt holdings are purchased for 20 or 30 cents for each dollar of debt outstanding. A successful investment outcome depends on restructuring distressed debt so that investors get more per dollar of debt than they paid—say 50 cents on the dollar. In other words, the return driver is not dependent on what is going on in the overall bond market, but on the ability of different constituents to reach an agreement.

MULTIPLE RETURN DRIVERS

Some investments have a combination of return drivers. For example, a real estate project might be economically viable without leverage, but the developer uses leverage to enhance the return. Another example is portable alpha, an investment strategy where an investment manager gets exposure to the stock market via futures and then actively invests the remaining capital in a different strategy or vehicle such as short-term bonds or even hedge fund strategies.

An investment's outcome is determined by the underlying drivers of performance. As investors, we can increase the odds of successful outcomes by allocating most of our capital to investments with dependable return drivers, such as income, cash flow growth, individual effort, and investments that can be purchased at attractive prices. Investments and speculations that require us to be precisely right or outsmart other investors are the least dependable return drivers. Successful portfolios have a diversified mix of return drivers.

CHAPTER SUMMARY

- In investing, there are no step-by-step instructions that can guarantee a successful outcome. Instead, we are wayfinders in that we have frames and rules of thumb that give us a sense we are heading in the right direction.

- Return drivers are an investment's attributes that determine its performance.

- Dependable return drivers include income, cash flow growth, and tradable factors such as dividend and value investing.

- Less dependable return drivers include leverage, the identification of individual mispriced securities, and speculation in non-income-generating assets such as gold and antiques.

- The consensus of investor opinion can be wrong such that the price of an individual stock doesn't reflect its intrinsic value. Sometimes investors are too optimistic about a company's prospect, and sometimes investors are too pessimistic.

- Usually these positive and negative surprises cancel each other, so that the overall stock market performance is driven by the dividend yield and the growth of that dividend over time.

- Successful portfolios have a diversified mix of dependable return drivers that the investor has identified beforehand. The investor knows that the drivers are what will determine investment success.

8

Who Is Getting a Cut?

Managing Fees and Taxes

THE TEN QUESTIONS

1. What is it?
2. Is it investing, speculating, or gambling?
3. What is the upside?
4. What is the downside?
5. Who is on the other side of the trade?
6. What is the investment vehicle?
7. What does it take to be successful?
8. **Who is getting a cut?**
9. How does it impact your portfolio?
10. Should you invest?

QUESTION EIGHT: WHO IS GETTING A CUT?

Successful investors are aware of the entities taking a portion of the return in the form of fees, expenses, and taxes. We should make sure we receive sufficient benefits for the fees we pay.

Earlier I shared how a listener to my podcast received a $1.5 million windfall when his employer issued stock to the public for the first time. The listener was trying to figure out what to do with this significant increase in wealth, so he hired a financial planner whose plan we analyzed. Twelve months later, the listener wrote: "I was optimistic enough to not listen to advice and [held] the majority of the shares, which [more than] doubled in value in the past year. The majority of my net worth ($2.4 million of about $4 million) is in [the] stock." He sold some shares to buy a new primary residence, and given how well the stock performed, he owed $700,000 in capital gains taxes from the shares he sold. He also used derivative contracts to protect his wealth in case the stock plummeted (which it eventually did). He wrote: "This probably means the value of my shares is actually $1.7 million if I subtract the tax liability. How do you reason about your net worth when there's always some tax liability?"[1]

The listener is correct that his net worth should be adjusted to reflect the tax liability. In investing, we often think of our investment gains as entirely our own, and then the government comes and takes some of those hard-earned profits away from us in the form of taxes. While it is appropriate to minimize our tax liability as much as possible, successful investing means paying taxes. It will be easier to pay them if we recognize that some of our investment gains were never really ours to begin with. The government is getting a portion.

The eighth question in our investing framework is, "Who is getting a cut?"—as in who is collecting a portion of our investment returns with regard to fees and taxes. Figuring out the cost of an investment can be challenging, as it is not always clear how much is being paid and to whom. I have had individuals tell me their broker doesn't charge them anything to manage their money. When I ask them to show me their portfolio, the holdings often include mutual funds that levy a commission or load when the fund is bought or sold. The mutual funds' expenses usually include an ongoing marketing/distribution fee, known as a 12b-1 fee, that is paid to the broker. While the broker might not charge an explicit advisory fee, he or she is being compensated.

TYPES OF INVESTMENT EXPENSES

Investment expenses can be categorized into three areas:

1. Trading costs
2. Advisory and management fees
3. Administrative fees

Sometimes these expenses are broken out, and at other times they are lumped together. For example, a mutual fund or ETF has an expense ratio that will include both management fees and administrative fees. A mutual fund might also charge an up-front sales load that could be considered a trading cost but is really compensation for the advisor. Some private investment partnerships will charge administrative costs such as tax preparation, legal, or even fund-raising expenses to the partnerships, and as investors we are sometimes not even aware of them. Let's take a look at these three expense categories in more detail.

Trading Costs

Trading costs are funds paid to a broker or advisor to enter or exit an investment. Sometimes these costs are explicit in terms of a trading commission to buy or sell stocks, while at other times the expenses are unseen, such as when a dealer or broker adds a markup to an individual bond before selling it to an investor. Trading costs also include the transaction fee that a broker might charge to purchase certain mutual funds.

The good news is in the past two decades individual investors have benefited from falling commission rates to purchase securities. Most brokerage firms now offer commission-free trades on hundreds of exchange-traded funds, and a number of brokerages offer commission-free trades on stocks and other securities. Brokerage firms that don't charge commissions on trades hope that clients will eventually use products or services that generate revenue for the firm. There are a number of ways brokerage firms can generate revenue besides commissions. Brokerages can be compensated for directing orders to trade execution services that will pay for the order flow. Brokerages earn fees through securities lending, which is the practice of allowing securities to be borrowed so investors can short and potentially profit from falling security prices. Brokerage firms also earn interest from margin loans, which are loans made to investors that want to use leverage to magnify their investment returns by buying securities with borrowed money. Some brokerages keep most of that margin loan interest income by paying zero or below-market interest rates on their customer's uninvested cash balances. These firms are able to keep a wide spread between what they earn on margin loans and what they pay out as interest on cash balances.

Advisory and Management Fees

Advisory and management fees are funds paid to professionals to manage specific investments. These include asset-based fees levied by a financial advisor to manage a client's portfolio. Management fees also include the fees that are deducted daily from mutual funds or ETFs that compensate the portfolio management team for overseeing the assets. These fees are part of the fund's or ETF's expense ratio and are detailed in the prospectus. Advisory fees include any commissions or loads to enter or exit an investment that compensate the investment advisor rather than the brokerage platform that executed the trade.

Similar to brokerage commissions, increased competition and improved technology have led to lower advisory fees and expense ratios. The Investment Company Institute reports that "in 2018, the average expense ratio of actively managed equity mutual funds fell to 0.76 percent, down from 1.04 percent in 1997. Index equity mutual fund expense ratios fell from 0.27 percent in 1997 to 0.08 percent in 2018." Index equity ETFs also saw a decline in expense ratios, falling to 0.20% in 2018 from 0.32% in 2009.[2]

Administrative Fees

Administrative fees compensate brokerage firms, fund companies, and retirement plan administrators for tracking investments, preparing and sending out statements and tax documents, and conducting other administrative tasks related to client account management.

MANAGING INVESTMENT FEES

Investment professionals and brokers deserve to be compensated fairly for their services. Yet as investors, we need to recognize that the investment costs we pay reduce our investment returns. During periods of low expected returns for stocks and bonds, investment fees can take a disproportionate cut of those returns. Consequently, we first need to be aware of what fees are being levied and then decide whether the fees justify the potential benefits.

For example, in Chapter 5, we saw how most active stock managers trail the overall stock market. Rather than pay an active stock manager or mutual fund 0.5% to 1.5% of assets annually when there is a high probability they will underperform their target benchmark, we can utilize an index mutual fund or ETF that seeks to replicate the target benchmark while often charging fees less than 0.15% of assets on an annual basis. Fidelity Investments even offers index mutual funds that have zero fees.[3]

If there is high probability that a manager can outperform a particular segment of the market net of fees, then perhaps an allocation to the manager makes sense. An actively managed fund may also be appropriate if there isn't a viable index fund or ETF option. For example, I am willing to pay an active bond manager to select non-investment-grade bonds rather than invest in a high-yield bond ETF because I believe the manager will be able to avoid companies that have a higher likelihood of defaulting on their bonds, thus generating better performance net of fees.

I also invest in closed-end funds. Closed-end funds have very high expenses, which is why I only purchase them when they are selling for an above-average discount to their net asset value. If the fund is selling at a 15% discount, then even after deducting a 2% expense ratio, it still might be a viable investment. For income-oriented closed-end funds, I always deduct the overall expense ratio from the closed-end fund's distribution yield to see what the potential income return will be after fees. A distribution yield is calculated by taking the most recent monthly or quarterly distribution and annualizing it. By deducting the annual expense ratio from the distribution yield, I can compare a closed-end fund with other investment options that might have lower expenses.

RETAINING A FINANCIAL ADVISOR

Should you hire a financial advisor to manage your portfolio for you? Is it worth the 0.8% or more that an advisor will charge to oversee your investments on a day-to-day basis? It depends on why you are hiring the manager. Many financial planners will work for a project fee or an hourly rate to prepare a comprehensive financial plan and make portfolio recommendations. Such advice can add significant value as you plan for retirement. After you review the financial plan, you could implement the portfolio recommendations on your own rather than pay the advisor an ongoing fee. Yet some individuals like the peace of mind of having an advisor oversee their portfolio on an ongoing basis. The advisor helps them keep their emotions in check during turbulent markets. Peace of mind is a valid reason to retain a financial advisor. Conversely, hiring an advisor because you expect the person to outperform the stock or bond markets through expert security selection is not a prudent reason to hire an investment advisor. Investment professionals with the skill and informational insight to outperform the market are rare. Truly skilled investment professionals gravitate to highly compensated areas such as managing a hedge fund. Successful hedge funds have very high account minimums of $10 million or more, or the funds have been closed to new investors for years.

A good financial advisor will provide perspective and collaborate with you as you prepare for and meet life's financial challenges. A good financial planner will also fully disclose the cost of his or her services and the fees of the underlying investments. A good financial planner will not promise to outperform the market, because very few will be able to fulfill that promise.

TAXES

Early in my investment career, one of my clients was a medical malpractice insurer. At times, I felt like I was in over my head with this client. The investment committee consisted mostly of physicians who were several decades older than me, and they viewed the investment world through a different perspective. They were very focused on both their portfolio's after-tax return and the way any investment activity would be reflected on the insurer's financial statements. Income was more highly prized than unrealized gains, even though income was taxed. Interest and dividend income were reflected as revenue on the company's income statement, whereas unrealized gains were not. One thing I liked about this client is the committee members met on Friday afternoons in Coral Gables, Florida, so I could take one of my kids with me and spend the weekend on the beach in the warm sunshine. Then the client merged with an insurer in Michigan, so our meetings were moved to Lansing.

Most of my clients to this point had been not-for-profits, so taxes were not a consideration, but this insurance client wanted me to calculate the portfolio's after-tax return in the quarterly report I would prepare. To do so, I would reduce the income the insurer received by the amount that went to taxes and lower the price appreciation to account for capital gains taxes. It was an extremely manual process, and through that exercise I became quite aware of how much taxes can reduce investment returns.

As individuals, the best way to minimize taxes is to only sell assets after they qualify for long-term capital gains treatment rather than the higher short-term capital gains rate. The most effective way to do that is to own exchange-traded funds rather than active mutual funds. The lower the portfolio turnover in terms of how frequently the underlying holdings of a fund or ETF are bought and sold, the more tax efficient a fund or ETF will be. An active mutual fund might sell a holding that it has held for less than a year if it appreciates rapidly and meets the manager's price target. Or a holding may be sold if the investment thesis changes. Under both scenarios, the security sale could result in a short-term capital gain that could be a taxable event for shareholders. An ETF will rarely sell a holding unless there is a change in the constituents in the underlying index the ETF tracks.

In addition, because ETF shares are redeemed when the ETF sponsor exchanges a basket of securities for ETF shares provided by authorized participants (as discussed in Chapter 6), there is an opportunity for the ETF sponsor to reduce the tax burden by transferring securities with a low cost basis to the authorized participant. A low cost basis means a security has appreciated a great deal in price and therefore would have a large taxable gain if it were sold.[4] Conversely, when there are large redemptions from an active mutual fund due to underperformance or as part of the ongoing trend of investors shifting to passive indexing vehicles from active mutual fund strategies, the mutual fund has to sell its existing holdings in the open market, potentially resulting in additional capital gains tax liability for the remaining shareholders.

As individual investors, we can also minimize our tax burden by taking advantage of tax-deferred savings vehicles and tax-free investments. Financial practitioners and academics generally agree that locating higher-yielding assets such as bonds and REITs in tax-deferred accounts and holding stocks in taxable accounts can reduce taxes and increase after-tax portfolio values. That is because the tax rate on dividends and interest for many individuals is higher than the capital gains tax rate. By locating higher-income investments in tax-deferred vehicles and high-growth, lower-income investments in taxable accounts, the annual tax burden is lower, allowing more time for asset balances to grow.[5]

I am not a tax expert, so there are much better sources including your tax accountant for fine-tuning your investment strategy as it relates to taxes. Your tax advisor can also provide insight about whether it makes sense to include some tax-free investments, such as municipal bonds, in your portfolio. Municipal bonds are debt securities issued by states, local governments, and school districts to fund various projects such as roads, utility infrastructure, and schools. Most municipal bonds are exempt from federal taxes and in many cases state and local taxes. Municipal bonds can be evaluated in the same way we analyzed bonds in Chapter 3 with a focus on yield, duration, and credit quality. The one adjustment with municipal bonds is that the yield needs to be put on an even playing field with taxable bonds by dividing the municipal bond's, fund's, or ETF's yield to maturity or SEC yield by 1 minus the investor's marginal tax rate.

For example, suppose a municipal bond fund has an SEC yield of 2.9%. For an investor with a 35% marginal tax rate, that is equivalent to a pretax yield of 4.5% (e.g., 2.9%/[1 − 35%] = 4.5%). The investor can then compare the tax-adjusted yield with the SEC yield of taxable bond funds with similar credit quality and interest rate sensitivity to see if it makes sense to invest.

REBALANCING YOUR PORTFOLIO

Another area in investing where costs come into play is in rebalancing an investment portfolio. Rebalancing consists of selling one asset that has performed well and is overweight relative to some target and allocating the proceeds to an asset that has not performed as well and is underweight relative to its target. Of course, this assumes there is an actual target for each investment or asset category, which may or may not be the case depending on your approach to asset allocation. We explore asset allocation in the next chapter.

As an institutional investment advisor, I had two types of clients. Some clients were nondiscretionary in that I made recommendations but ultimately the investment committee or staff had to make and implement decisions. The other clients were discretionary, in which case our portfolio management team would make and implement investment decisions.

For the nondiscretionary clients, rebalancing was an ongoing discussion. The decision to rebalance can be based on time as in, "We rebalance once per year." Or it could be based on threshold as in, "We rebalance every time an asset category is more than 20% away from its target." If it is a threshold decision, then an additional dimension is the frequency with which we look at the portfolio to see if an asset category is outside its target range.

For the not-for-profits I worked with, the cost of rebalancing was minimal since transaction fees were low and the entities didn't have to pay capital gains taxes. That is not true for individuals. I occasionally get e-mails from listeners who have held certain securities, such as individual stocks or index funds, in their taxable portfolios for years. These securities have a low cost basis, which means they will generate a large taxable gain if they are sold as part of a rebalancing strategy. In a case where there is a large tax liability, the dollar cost of rebalancing including taxes and transaction fees needs to be weighed against the potential benefit. Three questions to ask are (1) how much do you need to earn with the new investment to offset the cost of selling the old one, (2) how long would it take to recoup that cost, and (3) what would the financial harm be if the existing holding plummets in value? This third question is especially relevant where there is an individual stock that constitutes a large percentage of an investment portfolio.

Concerning which rebalancing strategy is preferred, there isn't a right answer. Yan Zilbering, Colleen M. Jaconetti, and Francis M. Kinniry, Jr., prepared a paper for Vanguard on best practices for rebalancing portfolios. Based on their analysis, they determined that the frequency of portfolio rebalancing, be it monthly, quarterly, or annually, did not meaningfully impact risk-adjusted returns. They found, however, the number of rebalancing events increases cost. They concluded "that a rebalancing strategy based on reasonable monitoring frequencies (such as annual or semiannual) and reasonable allocation thresholds (variations of 5% or so) is likely to provide sufficient risk control relative to the target asset allocation for most portfolios with broadly diversified stock and bond holdings, without creating too many rebalancing events over the long term."[6]

For my discretionary clients where the portfolio management team and I made and implemented the investment decisions, we didn't have a lot of formal discussion regarding rebalancing. These clients had fairly wide ranges around their specific asset category targets, and as investment managers our charge was to make prudent portfolio decisions based on investment conditions. We would adjust the portfolio mix incrementally when the client added or redeemed funds or when investment conditions changed. We would sell a portion of an asset category that needed to be trimmed because it had performed well and had lower return prospects, and we would add to asset categories that were less expensive than their historical average and had higher expected returns. It was a more fluid portfolio management approach rather than a rigid rebalancing approach that assumes there is an optimal portfolio target that needed to be closely followed. That is how I continue to manage my own portfolio today.

INFLATION AND ASSET ALLOCATION

So far in this chapter we have covered explicit investment costs such as fees and taxes. Inflation is an additional cost that is not disclosed in a prospectus or brokerage agreement because it is not levied by a financial services firm. Inflation is the loss of purchasing power due to the rise in prices over time. Inflation is caused when the supply of money increases faster than the supply of goods and services. Most of the money supply increase comes from banks issuing new loans. Investors should be aware of the current inflation rate as measured by the consumer price index and whether their investments are earning more than that rate. The incremental return earned above inflation is called a real return. We need to earn a positive real return in order to offset the loss of purchasing power due to inflation.

For example, college endowments will generally have a minimum target rate of return that equals the percentage amount they withdraw from their portfolios annually plus the rate of inflation. If their annual spending rate is 4% and the expected inflation rate is 3%, then their minimum target return would be 7%. If they meet this return target and inflation comes in at the 3% expectation and spending is at 4% per year, then the financial impact of what the endowments spend 20 years from now will be the same as it is today after adjusting for inflation. If the endowment earns more than 7%, generating a positive real return net of spending, then the financial impact of what is spent 20 years from now will be higher than today.

We can do a similar analysis as individual investors. If we keep our portfolios in cash equivalents that yield less than inflation, then the value of our assets on an inflation-adjusted basis will shrink because our portfolio will have a negative real return. Conversely, a 100% stock portfolio will most likely generate a positive real return over the long term, but it can also go through periods where it generates negative real returns. If stocks fall 60%, then that could cause significant financial harm for an investor in or near retirement. Portfolio management is the process of combining multiple asset categories that contribute to a positive real portfolio return while minimizing the financial harm caused by major market drawdowns. To better understand the impact of inflation, it can be helpful to use a spreadsheet that allows you to compare a future portfolio value and spending amount with what they would be worth in today's dollars. You can do that by downloading my retirement savings spreadsheet and watching a video that explains how to use it. You can find those resources at https://moneyfortherestofus.com/tools.

HOW TO MANAGE INVESTMENT COSTS IN YOUR PORTFOLIO

All investment costs including trading costs, advisory fees, administrative fees, taxes, and inflation reduce our investment returns. These costs can't be avoided, but they can be effectively managed. The starting point is understanding what costs you are paying and deciding if you are receiving sufficient benefit. Is there a way to reduce costs to increase your after-tax, net-of-fee returns? Often there are other options, given that investment costs continue to decline and tax-efficient options are available, such as exchange-traded funds. When contemplating portfolio changes, you should also calculate the dollar cost of exiting a position in terms of fees and taxes and determine how long it will take the new investment opportunity to earn back those costs.

For work-sponsored defined contribution plans, you can determine the costs of the different portfolio options and focus your investing on the lower-cost ones. You can then complement those investments with your after-tax savings, keeping in mind the tax-savings strategy of locating higher-income-generating investments within tax-deferred savings vehicles.

CHAPTER SUMMARY

- Investment expenses can be categorized into trading costs, advisory fees, and administrative fees. These fees lower our investment returns, so we need to make sure we are getting sufficient benefits, and if not, seek out lower-cost options.

- Good financial advisors will provide perspective and collaborate with you as you prepare for and meet life's financial challenges. They will fully disclose the cost of their services and the fees of the underlying investments. They will not promise to outperform the market, because very few will be able to fulfill that promise.

- Successful investing means paying taxes, but we can also take steps to minimize them.

- Rebalancing consists of selling one asset that has performed well and is overweight relative to some target and allocating the proceeds to an asset that has not performed as well and is underweight relative to its target. Rebalancing can be triggered based on an asset exceeding a certain percentage threshold, or it can be based on a set time schedule. A more flexible approach where there are no formal asset class targets is to adjust the portfolio mix incrementally when adding or withdrawing funds or as investment conditions change.

- Individual investors can overcome the hidden cost of inflation by combining asset categories that contribute to a positive real portfolio return.

9

How Does It Impact Your Portfolio?

Asset Allocation

THE TEN QUESTIONS

1. What is it?
2. Is it investing, speculating, or gambling?
3. What is the upside?
4. What is the downside?
5. Who is on the other side of the trade?
6. What is the investment vehicle?
7. What does it take to be successful?
8. Who is getting a cut?
9. **How does it impact your portfolio?**
10. Should you invest?

QUESTION NINE: HOW DOES IT IMPACT YOUR PORTFOLIO?

A diversified portfolio consists of a variety of asset categories with different return drivers. We shouldn't approach asset allocation as an optimization problem with a single right answer. Rather, using guidelines and rules of thumb, we have tremendous creative freedom to build an investment portfolio that aligns with our knowledge, interests, and values.

Most of the questions in our framework analyze individual investments on a stand-alone basis. Yet investments are not bought in isolation. They contribute to the return of our overall investment portfolio. The ninth question in the framework considers this component by asking, "How does it impact your portfolio?" As portfolio managers, we make allocation decisions among different investment opportunities. How do we decide what assets to include and how much money to allocate to them?

ASSET ALLOCATION USING MODERN PORTFOLIO THEORY

The traditional asset allocation approach is based on modern portfolio theory (MPT). This financial theory was introduced by Harry Markowitz in 1952 and was expanded upon from the early 1950s through the early 1970s. Markowitz won the Nobel Prize in 1990 for his efforts, and modern portfolio theory remains the bedrock of modern finance. The idea behind modern portfolio theory is that for a given level of risk, there is an optimal portfolio mix (i.e., the split between stocks, bonds, real estate, and other asset classes) that maximizes the expected return. With MPT, risk is defined as volatility, which is the variability of returns around the average or expected return. How high are the highs compared with how low are the lows. Standard deviation is the statistical measure used to estimate volatility in asset allocation models based on MPT.

In order to produce an asset allocation study using MPT, for each asset class you need an expected return and an expected volatility. You also need an assumption for how those asset classes move in relation to each other. How closely do the asset class returns track in the same direction or perhaps move in the opposite direction? This is called correlation.

With these inputs, the optimization model calculates the optimal mix between stocks, bonds, real estate, and other asset classes that maximizes the expected return for a given level of volatility. A line graph of the optimal portfolios, those with the highest expected return for each level of volatility, is called an efficient frontier.

As an institutional investment advisor, when I began working with a new university endowment client or other not-for-profit, I would present an asset allocation study based on modern portfolio theory. The goal of the exercise was for the client to select an optimal portfolio mix that resided on the efficient frontier. This optimal portfolio needed to earn a sufficient return to allow the client to have adequate spending today while ensuring sufficient capital to spend a similar or greater amount on an inflation-adjusted basis in perpetuity. At the same time, the expected return couldn't be so high that the investment committee and other stakeholders were unable to withstand the short-term downside volatility a higher-risk portfolio could experience.

For individuals saving for retirement, typically the goal is to identify an optimal portfolio that allows them to compound their existing and future savings at a rate that provides sufficient assets to fund their living expenses during retirement. Yet that expected return can't be so high that the individual is unable to withstand the volatility. Otherwise, they might dump risky assets in a panic during or after a major market downturn.

The output from an asset allocation study is highly dependent on the inputs. In Chapter 3, I was critical of a financial advisor who created a financial plan based on historical returns. While it is acceptable to use historical volatility numbers and correlations, using historical asset class returns to support portfolio recommendations can be misleading. Especially if, as we saw in earlier chapters, the starting investment conditions, such as current bond yields, dividend yields, or valuations, suggest history will be unlikely to repeat.

Early in my investment career, the asset allocation model we used was completely based on historical returns. I could choose any historical time period I wanted, and the model would generate an efficient frontier based on the historical returns, volatilities, and correlations. Given this flexibility, I would cherry-pick the time period that gave me historical returns that seemed reasonable for what might happen in the future. Still, I was shocked at how shifting the historical time period by a year or two dramatically changed the model's output.

More importantly, I found in presenting asset allocation studies to clients that they didn't really want an optimal portfolio. They wanted one that fit their comfort level. Consequently I would add constraints to the model such as no more than 15% in small-company stocks or 20% in non-U.S. stocks. My recommended portfolios were "optimal" in the sense that they were palatable to the client. They indeed resided on an efficient frontier, but only because the frontier was heavily customized to the client's comfort level. On more than one occasion I even increased the size of the dots on the graph that represented portfolio recommendations so they touched the efficient frontier line. This process was very much an exercise in creating an "optimal" diet for clients consisting of food groups they were willing to eat, rather than the healthiest food groups for them.

A few years later, we began using an asset allocation model based on forward-looking return assumptions instead of backward-looking ones. I eventually stopped showing efficient frontiers altogether, because it seemed like such a farce given all the constraints I would place on the curve in order to show portfolios I thought clients would find agreeable.

Problems with Modern Portfolio Theory

Now, I don't use MPT in my personal investing. While I embrace diversified multi–asset class portfolios, I find that relying on the output of an asset allocation model based on modern portfolio theory gives some investors a false sense of confidence regarding portfolio outcomes. The problem with MPT is that it assumes market returns congregate around the average expected return much more than they actually do. In other words, the theory assumes that exceptionally good or bad returns are extremely rare. Yet catastrophic losses happen more frequently than what the theory suggests.

Mathematician Benoit Mandelbrot was one of the first to point out that extreme portfolio outcomes happen with greater frequency than MPT models predict. In addition, these extreme events tend to clump together rather than be spread out randomly, just like when flying on an airplane, a jolt due to air turbulence tends to be followed by another and another until eventually a period of smoother flight ensues. In financial markets, one period of high volatility tends to be followed by another, at which point markets calm for a time before getting more volatile again.[1]

Why is this important? Because with MPT, investors and their advisors tend to focus on the average expected return rather than their exposure to extreme events. Nassim Nicholas Taleb explains it this way: "Risks are seen in tail events rather than in the variations."[2] As individual investors, our primary measure of risk shouldn't be volatility, or "variations," as Taleb puts it. Volatility and standard deviation are too abstract. Risk for individuals is the financial harm caused by extreme events, large losses that happen more frequently than what optimization models based on modern portfolio theory predict. These extreme negative outcomes are the tail events Taleb refers to. They are called tail events because in a plot of possible outcomes known as a probability distribution, extreme outcomes are observations that occur in the tails or ends of the distribution rather than near the average where the bulk of the observations occur.

Most people already make some financial decisions with an eye toward extreme events. On average, your house won't burn down or be robbed, and yet you carry homeowners insurance. On average, you won't die or be incapacitated in the prime of your life, and yet you buy life and disability insurance to protect your family. In these examples, the extreme events are rare, so insurance premiums are affordable. That is not the case with financial markets. Seeking to hedge or protect a portfolio against losses through the use of option contracts or other means is expensive, which is further evidence that MPT underestimates the frequency and severity of extreme outcomes. Otherwise it would be more affordable to hedge against portfolio losses.

Granted, volatility can be a useful guide in that asset classes that are more volatile tend to experience greater losses, but rather than focus on standard deviation, I think it is more instructive to focus on the maximum potential drawdown (i.e., loss) and the potential recovery period as we discussed in Chapter 4.

Another problem with MPT is the models assume the correlation between asset classes is static in that two asset classes that are not perfectly correlated will not start moving in lockstep with each other. Unfortunately, during periods of market turmoil, the correlation between asset classes often increases; riskier assets such as different categories of stocks, REITs, and non-investment-grade bonds all decline in price together.

Yet another challenge with modern portfolio theory is some asset categories are illiquid, so they are not priced every day. What is the volatility of a rental apartment? There is very little volatility on a daily or monthly basis, because apartment buildings are not priced or valued every day. They are only appraised every few years. Consequently, investment advisors that produce asset allocation studies using MPT are forced to invent volatility and correlation assumptions for illiquid investments such as private real estate or venture capital, which are privately owned start-up companies.

My biggest issue with modern portfolio theory, however, is that it's just too tidy. It simplifies the investing world too much, suggesting a model can adequately capture potential portfolio outcomes in the face of extreme uncertainty. Financial markets are complex adaptive systems with a wide variety of inputs that adapt and learn over time. Millions of individual agents, both human and computer, take actions that impact the economy and financial markets in ways that are unpredictable. Ben Hunt, chief investment officer at the investment boutique Second Foundation and author of the *Epsilon Theory* newsletter, writes:

> Everything that Modern Portfolio Theory tells you is based on decision-making under risk. It's all an exercise in *maximization*— maximizing your expected return over a series of risk vs. reward decisions—and that works out perfectly well if you have stable historical data and well-defined current risks. Less well if you have unstable historical data and poorly defined current risks....
>
> ... It's like using a saw when you need a hammer. Not only do you have no chance of driving in that nail, but you're going to damage the wood.[3]

Maximizing our wealth is not the goal of investing or asset allocation. Hunt says the goal is to "minimize [our] maximum regret" in the long term.[4] That means we should invest in a way that builds wealth over time while avoiding big bets that can leave us financially destitute. It means not coming under the spell of "phantastic"[5] investment opportunities that promise high returns with little risk, enticing us to sell most of what we possess and putting it in cryptocurrencies, a start-up company, or a hot stock so that we are significantly harmed if things don't go as planned.[6]

THE ASSET GARDEN APPROACH TO ASSET ALLOCATION

Given the challenges with modern portfolio theory, how do we choose an asset mix in a world of uncertainty? We start with an understanding that there isn't a right answer, no "optimal" portfolio. Mervyn King, former governor of the Bank of England, wrote: "The language of optimisation is seductive. But humans do not optimise; they cope. They respond and adapt to new surroundings, new stimuli and new challenges."[7] King points out that we cope with problems that don't lend themselves to optimization by using heuristics or rules of thumb, such as the rules of thumb for estimating the return potential of different investment strategies.

One way to do this with asset allocation is to approach it like landscaping a yard or a garden. When landscaping, there isn't a correct answer. There isn't an optimized flower garden. Instead, the landscaper plants dozens of varieties of grasses, bushes, and flowers comprising different colors, leaf shapes, and heights. Plants that bloom at different times, that are resistant to different diseases, some that bear edible fruit, some that are more drought tolerant, some annuals, perennials, etc. There are rules of thumb or principles that a gardener follows given the regional climate, but there is also a huge leeway for artistic interpretation.

Likewise, we want a variety of asset classes in our portfolio that have differing characteristics and return drivers. Like a landscaper, there are guidelines and rules of thumb to follow, but there is tremendous creative freedom to build an investment portfolio that aligns with our knowledge, interests, and values.

The initial building blocks of any asset allocation are cash and stocks. Cash is the base layer where we get a little bit of income with very low risk of loss in principal. Unfortunately, in most market environments the yield on cash and cash equivalents, such as bank savings accounts, money market mutual funds, or bank certificate of deposits, barely keeps up with inflation. That means cash balances are not growing after adjusting for rising prices. They might even be losing money on an inflation-adjusted basis. That is why most investors will want to add a stock allocation to their portfolio. Not only do stocks have an income yield like cash in the form of dividends, but that dividend cash flow grows as corporate earnings grow. Stocks over the long term have outperformed inflation, but they also can suffer from severe losses as investors adjust what they are willing to pay for that cash flow stream as reflected in changing price-to-earnings ratios.

You don't need modern portfolio theory to determine your allocation to stocks versus cash. You just need a simple spreadsheet with the current yield for cash as well as the expected return, maximum drawdown, and time to recover for stocks.

We can develop an expected return or upside for stocks using the three rules of thumb of cash flow, cash flow growth, and the potential change in what investors are paying for that cash flow. I usually start with an estimate for global stocks that includes both U.S. and non-U.S. stocks. In our example, let's use a dividend yield of 2.4% for the cash flow component and 4.1% earnings per share growth for the cash flow growth component. Our time frame will be ten years. We will assume that the price-to-earnings ratio for global stocks is in line with its long-term average, so we won't make any adjustment to our expected return related to investors changing what they are willing to pay for cash flow growth. That means our ten-year expected return for stocks is 6.5%, the sum of the 2.4% dividend yield plus the 4.1% earnings per share growth rate.

We also need an estimate for the downside for stocks based on their maximum historical losses and how long it has taken in the past to recover from those losses. The maximum drawdown for the MSCI All Country World Index (ACWI), a global stock index comprising 23 developed markets and 24 emerging markets countries, was 58.4%.[8] This occurred during the 2008 global financial crisis. Let's round up and assume a 60% maximum drawdown and that it takes 48 months, or 4 years, to recover those losses.

For the estimated return for cash, let's use 2.5% and assume 2.5% will also be the annual inflation rate. With those inputs, we can calculate the expected return for a given stock-cash allocation by multiplying the percentage allocation to stocks by the stock's expected return and the percentage allocation to cash by the cash's expected return. For example, given the expected return of 6.5% for stocks and 2.5% for cash, a portfolio that is 60% stocks and 40% cash would have an expected return of 4.9%. The calculation is (60% stock allocation × 6.5% stock return) + (40% cash allocation × 2.5% cash return) = 4.9%.

If stocks have a maximum drawdown of 60% and a recovery period of 48 months, then a portfolio with 60% allocated to stocks would have an estimated maximum drawdown of 36% (i.e., 60% stock allocation × 60% drawdown = 36%). It would also have an estimated recovery period of approximately 29 months (i.e., 60% stock allocation × 48 months recovery = 28.8 months). (See Table 9.1.)

TABLE 9.1 Stock and Cash Portfolio Example

Dividend yield (dividend/price)	2.4%
Earnings per share growth	4.1%
Expected stocks return (earning growth + dividend yield)	6.5%
Expected cash return	2.5%
Portfolio return for 60% stocks and 40% cash*	4.9%
Maximum drawdown (60% stock allocation x 60% drawdown)	36.0%
Estimated recovery period (60% stock allocation x 48 months recovery)	28.8 months

*(60% stock allocation x 6.5% stock return) + (40% cash allocation x 2.5% cash return)

Is that an appropriate allocation? It depends on the personal financial harm a 36% loss could cause. Would it change your lifestyle? Is your portfolio relatively small, and do you have many years until you retire, so you have plenty of time to recoup losses? Or are you near retirement age, and such a devastating loss would force you to postpone your retirement?

Once you determine the maximum drawdown you are comfortable with, you can seek to improve the expected return by adding additional asset classes. Perhaps you want to increase your portfolio's expected return by investing in bonds instead of cash, given bonds typically have a higher yield. You can do so by evaluating the yield to maturity or yield to worst of different bond offerings. In the United States, you can evaluate the SEC yield for ETF and fund options to see how much additional yield you can get compared with cash. Then you evaluate whether that yield is worth the additional interest rate risk in terms of the potential price decline for the bond offerings if interest rates rise. You do so by comparing the duration of the various options as we discussed in Chapter 3. You should also evaluate the bond offering's credit risk and how much incremental yield or spread you get for corporate bonds relative to U.S. Treasuries compared to the historical average spread.

In our example, let's assume a 3.5% 10-year expected return for U.S. investment-grade bonds with an expected maximum drawdown of 5% and a 12-month recovery period. These are conservative assumptions, because usually when global stocks sell off, interest rates fall, which leads to higher bond prices. In calculating the expected maximum loss and recovery periods in the portfolio examples that follow, I assume that the stock and bond losses occur simultaneously.

A three-asset-class portfolio using global stocks, U.S. bonds, and cash provides a solid investing foundation (see Table 9.2). Such a portfolio could be implemented using two low-cost ETFs or index mutual funds and a money market mutual fund. Some investors stop there, and that is perfectly fine. Others prefer an asset garden with more variety that has additional return drivers.

TABLE 9.2 Portfolio Example Assumptions

	Expected Return	Maximum Drawdown	Recovery Period
Global stocks	6.5%	60%	48 months
U.S. investment-grade bonds	3.5%	5%	12 months
Cash	2.5%	0%	0 months

Before looking at additional asset category options, let's review some examples of portfolios with three asset classes using our assumptions along with who might use these portfolios.

Ultraconservative Portfolio Example

An ultraconservative portfolio (Table 9.3) might be appropriate for:

■ Investors in or nearing retirement/financial independence whose spending plans and lifestyle would be *severely disrupted* by a major market downturn. In other words, investors who can't afford to lose much money, but understand that a *very low tolerance for risk* will require a lower return objective.

■ Investors, including retirees, who have sufficient investment assets or pensions to meet their spending needs while earning a very low return on their investment portfolio. In other words, investors who can maintain their lifestyle without taking much investment risk.

TABLE 9.3   An Ultraconservative Portfolio

Global stocks	20%
U.S. investment-grade bonds	60%
Cash	20%
Expected return	3.9%
Expected excess return over inflation	1.4%
Expected maximum drawdown	−15.0%
Expected recovery period	17 months

Conservative Portfolio Example

A conservative portfolio (Table 9.4) might be appropriate for:

■ Investors in or nearing retirement/financial independence whose spending plans and lifestyle would be *disrupted* by a major market downturn. In other words, investors who can't afford to lose much money, but understand that a *low tolerance for risk* will require a lower return objective.

- Investors, including retirees, who have sufficient investment assets or pensions to meet their spending needs while earning a low return on their investment portfolio. In other words, investors who can maintain their lifestyle without taking much investment risk.

TABLE 9.4   A Conservative Portfolio

Global stocks	40%
U.S. investment-grade bonds	45%
Cash	15%
Expected return	4.6%
Expected excess return over inflation	2.1%
Expected maximum drawdown	−26.3%
Expected recovery period	25 months

Moderate Portfolio Example

A moderate portfolio (Table 9.5) might be appropriate for:

- Investors who are continuing to save for retirement/financial independence and whose spending plans and lifestyle would *not be majorly disrupted* by a large market downturn.
- Investors who will be retiring within the next 10 to 15 years and have a moderate toleration for risk in terms of the level of portfolio losses they can withstand without panicking.

TABLE 9.5   A Moderate Portfolio

Global stocks	60%
U.S. investment-grade bonds	30%
Cash	10%
Expected return	5.2%
Expected excess return over inflation	2.7%
Expected maximum drawdown	−37.5%
Expected recovery period	32 months

Moderately Aggressive Portfolio Example

A moderately aggressive portfolio (Table 9.6) might be appropriate for:

- Investors who are continuing to save for retirement/financial independence and whose spending plans and lifestyle would *not be disrupted* by a large market downturn.
- Investors who will be retiring within the next 15 to 25 years and have a moderately aggressive toleration for risk with regard to the level of portfolio losses they can withstand without panicking.

TABLE 9.6   A Moderately Aggressive Portfolio

Global stocks	75%
U.S. investment-grade bonds	20%
Cash	5%
Expected return	5.7%
Expected excess return over inflation	3.2%
Expected maximum drawdown	–46%
Expected recovery period	38 months

Aggressive Portfolio Example

An aggressive portfolio (Table 9.7) might be appropriate for:

- Investors who are continuing to save for retirement/financial independence and whose spending plans and lifestyle would *not be disrupted* by a large market downturn.
- Investors who will not be retiring for another 25 years or more and are extremely tolerant toward risk in terms of their ability to withstand large portfolio losses without panicking.
- Investors who want to achieve higher portfolio returns through a significant allocation to stocks.

TABLE 9.7 An Aggressive Portfolio

Global stocks	85%
U.S. investment-grade bonds	15%
Cash	0%
Expected return	6.1%
Expected excess return over inflation	3.6%
Expected maximum drawdown	–51.8%
Expected recovery period	43 months

These portfolio examples show the expected excess return over inflation. To better understand the impact of inflation, it can be helpful to use a spreadsheet that allows you to compare a future portfolio value and spending amount with what they would be worth in today's dollars. You can do that by downloading my retirement savings spreadsheet and watching a video that explains how to use it. You can find those resources at https://moneyfortherestofus.com/tools. Understanding the impact of large portfolio losses can also help you in selecting a portfolio mix. You can model that by using the retirement spending spreadsheet at https://moneyfortherestofus.com/tools.

Once your three-asset-class portfolio foundation is in place, you can complement it with additional asset categories you have analyzed using our ten-question framework. Asset categories that are more stocklike in terms of their maximum potential drawdown can be included in the higher-risk stock bucket. For example, you might want to add an allocation to real estate investment trusts or to faster-growing small-company stocks. Asset categories that are more yield oriented such as high-yield bonds could be included as part of the bond and cash allocation. You may want to include some private, less liquid assets in your portfolio such as rental real estate. Private investments provide pockets of independence away from the public financial markets, and because they are not priced daily, they offer some peace of mind and stability when the public markets are especially volatile. For example, perhaps you decide to add a small speculation in gold coins or antiques to your portfolio.

Again, there is not an optimal asset mix, just as there isn't an optimal garden. We simply add investments that we believe will enhance the variety or diversification in our portfolio. These are investments that we analyze using our ten-question framework so that we can explain what they are, their potential upside and downside, who is on the other side of the trade, and what it will it take for the investment to be successful, as well as what the fees are, whether they are appropriate, and how liquid the investments are.

I have over a dozen asset classes in my personal portfolio, and I have not run an asset allocation study using modern portfolio theory in years. Table 9.8 shows a summary of my personal investment portfolio.

In my portfolio, I add investments when they have an attractive expected return and reduce their exposure when I feel like I am no longer being adequately compensated for the risk. It is a more fluid and flexible approach than using MPT. That flexibility is your competitive advantage as an individual investor. Jeremy Grantham, cofounder and chief investment strategist at the investment firm GMO, wrote, "The individual is far better-positioned to wait patiently for the right pitch while paying no regard to what others are doing, which is almost impossible for professionals."[9]

Investment advisors and financial planners use MPT-based asset allocation models and risk questionnaires in making recommendations to their clients because they are managing hundreds of accounts. Those tools allow them to efficiently oversee multiple portfolios by categorizing clients by their risk tolerance. As an individual investor, you aren't managing hundreds of portfolios, so you don't have to adhere to a rigid asset allocation framework like MPT. You can adapt and customize your portfolio over time as you analyze new investment opportunities using the ten-question framework. I often start out with a smaller position size if it is a new investment, so I can get comfortable with how it performs and make sure I have a good understanding of its characteristics.

TABLE 9.8 David's Portfolio

Asset Category	What Is It?	Portfolio Percentage
Global stocks	Equity ownership via ETFs and funds	9%
REITs	Publicly traded real estate holdings via ETFs	3%
Preferred stock	Equity ownership with fixed dividends	1%
Master limited partnerships	Energy infrastructure assets	3%
YieldCos	Renewable energy infrastructure assets	1%
Bonds	Fixed-income securities via ETFs and funds	10%
Bank loans	Floating-rate leveraged loans via a mutual fund	1%
Private real estate	Real estate and land holdings	27%
Private capital	Leveraged buyout, venture capital, and real asset funds	11%
Asset-based lending	Loans made to individuals secured by real estate	21%
Unsecured lending	Unsecured loans made to individuals	1%
Art and antiques	Furniture and paintings	1%
Gold	Primarily gold coins and one gold ETF	4%
Cryptocurrencies	Bitcoin, Ethereum, Litecoin, and others	1%
Cash	Assets held at banks or other cash equivalents	6%
		100%

An additional advantage of not investing as if there is an optimal or correct portfolio is it is much easier to make changes. We are less fearful about making incremental changes if we treat our portfolio mix more like a garden rather than an optimized target. If flower gardens were optimized, we would be afraid to pull out a plant for fear of disrupting the artistic balance. Likewise, the emotional stakes are lower when it comes to investing if we approach our portfolio mix as layers of asset classes with different return drivers that can be adjusted as conditions change.

INTERNATIONAL STOCKS AND BONDS

As an investment advisor, I found that asset allocation studies based on modern portfolio theory were extremely effective at convincing clients to shift some of their U.S. stock allocation to non-U.S. stocks. By assuming that the U.S. and non-U.S. stock markets were not perfectly correlated, I demonstrated to my clients that allocating 10% to 20% of their assets to non-U.S. stocks lowered the portfolio's expected volatility for a given level of return. The client would select a non-U.S. equity allocation target based on the analysis, and if the client didn't already have a non-U.S. stock manager, we would assist in choosing one. Why did I recommend a 10% to 20% allocation to non-U.S. stocks? Because I knew that was what the client would be comfortable with, so I constrained the efficient frontier so that it only showed optimal portfolios with an international stock allocation of less than 20%.

Given that I just pointed out the flaws of modern portfolio theory including the fact that correlations aren't static and tend to increase during market downturns, why bother investing in international stocks? Is it worth doing so, particularly if the diversification benefit of investing outside your home country might not be there when you need it most, when stocks are falling? If modern portfolio theory is flawed, then it is difficult to use it to justify investing outside one's home country.

John Bogle, founder of the Vanguard Group, and whom some consider the father of indexing, said, "You don't need to own international stock."[10] Bogle reasoned that international stocks are riskier due to currency risk, economic risk, and societal instability risk. He didn't think investors were compensated for those risks in terms of higher returns. Plus many companies sell their products outside their home market so investors can benefit from a growing global economy without having to invest outside their home country.

Yet Bogle was also a strong proponent of indexing, which is based on the assumption that stocks are correctly priced in that every stock reflects its intrinsic value, the present value of its future dividend stream. Consequently, efficient market advocates believe it is a waste of time to identify mispriced securities, so investors are better off passively owning the market via index funds or ETFs. But how do we define the market? Is the market just the 500 U.S. stocks that compose the S&P 500 Index? Or is it all U.S. stocks? Why wouldn't the market also include non-U.S. stocks?

If all stocks are priced correctly, then their weighting within the overall market must be correct. By weighting, I am referring to a publicly traded company's market capitalization, which is the number of stock shares outstanding multiplied by the price. Most index funds are capitalization weighted in that the percentage allocated to a particular stock is based on its overall size, which is a function of its price and the number of shares outstanding.

For example, in November 2018, Apple was the largest company in the world, with a market capitalization of approximately $1 trillion. Apple had 4.8 billion stock shares outstanding. If we multiply 4.8 billion shares by Apple's stock price, which was $210 at the time, we get a market capitalization of $1 trillion.[11] A similar calculation can be done for all publicly traded stocks in the United States and the world. The sum of the individual stock market capitalizations equals the market capitalization of the overall market. Earlier in this chapter, I referred to the MSCI All Country World Index, which comprises 23 developed markets and 24 emerging markets countries. The ACWI contains 2,791 holdings and covers approximately 85% of the world's investable stocks. In November 2018, the sum of the market capitalizations that composed the ACWI equaled $46.8 trillion. Apple made up just over 2% of the ACWI, as

Apple's $1 trillion capitalization divided by $46.8 trillion capitalization for the overall market is approximately 2%. The sum of all the U.S. companies included in the ACWI equals approximately 55% of the world's market capitalization. That means investors who choose to invest only in the United States are avoiding 45% of the world's stocks as measured by capitalization.[12]

Here then is the inconsistency between investing only in the U.S. stock market and being a strong advocate for efficient markets and passive investing. If stocks are priced correctly, then their prices should reflect economic, societal, and political risks. That means riskier stocks should be priced to outperform less risky stocks in order to compensate investors for the added risk. A passive investor that ignores 45% of the world's stocks by investing only in U.S. index funds is taking a very active bet that the U.S. stock market will consistently outperform the rest of the world when in theory the rest of the world should outperform the U.S. stock market if indeed the rest of the world is riskier. True passive investors will own a global portfolio of stocks weighted by market capitalization. Granted, investing outside one's home country does involve currency risk, as currencies fluctuate, but investors can eliminate that risk by purchasing passive global ETFs that hedge out the currency risk.

I don't believe financial markets are perfectly efficient. Collectively, market participants can be wrong, which results in a systematic overvaluation or undervaluation of asset classes or subsegments of the market. Consequently, for my stock allocation the base layer consists of passive global stock ETFs, some hedged for currency risk and some unhedged. Then I add to that base layer by investing in segments of the stock market I believe offer an expected return greater than the global stock market because either dividend yields are higher, earnings growth is expected to be higher, or valuations as measured by price-to-earnings ratio are lower.

Conversely, most of my bond allocation is in U.S. bonds because most developed non-U.S. bond markets have a lower yield than the U.S. bond market, which means the expected returns are lower. I sometimes invest in emerging markets bonds when the yields are attractive, but I tend to focus on dollar-denominated emerging markets bonds so I don't have to worry about fluctuations in currency exchange rates.

FUNDAMENTAL INDEXING

ETFs and index mutual funds that are capitalization weighted are highly efficient for fund sponsors to manage in that they don't require much trading to adjust positions sizes. As a result, they tend to have the lowest costs in terms of expense ratios. A capitalization-weighted index fund or ETF rarely has to rebalance its security holdings due to market fluctuations, because as the prices of individual stocks rise or fall, their weight in the fund will always equal the weight in the index it seeks to track since the index is weighted by size. In contrast, an ETF that weights its holdings equally has to periodically rebalance in order to get its stocks back at equal weight.

Why would an ETF or index fund choose a weighting scheme that isn't capitalization weighted? For example, a fundamentally weighted index fund or ETF weights its holdings not by size but by other metrics such as revenue, earnings, dividend yield, etc. Fundamental indexing is an example of smart beta that we covered in Chapter 7. The only reason to pursue a non-capitalization-weighted investment strategy is if stock markets are inefficient in that the prices of stocks are not always correct. Rob Arnott of Research Affiliates, who helped develop the concept of fundamental indexing, pointed out that because capitalization-weighted indices and funds are weighted by size, which is a function of price, then by definition any stock that is priced higher than its intrinsic value will have an outsized position in the capitalization-weighted index than if it is priced correctly. A stock that is priced lower than its intrinsic value will have too small a weight in a capitalization-weighted index. Therefore, investment strategies that systematically weight their holdings in a way that differs from a capitalization-weighted index have a contrarian bias that can lead to excess returns relative to a capitalization-weighted index. As part of their rebalancing, these non-capitalization-weighted strategies will sell stocks that have done well and are now a bigger part of a capitalization-weighted index and potentially too expensive and buy stocks that have not done as well and are potentially undervalued. Arnott said: "Whether you are equal weighting or fundamental index or minimum variance, you're going to be having an anchor, a target weight that isn't related to price. So whether the price soars and tumbles, you're going to be selling and buying, it's a built-in structural sell high buy low discipline."[13] Fundamental indexing benefits over the long term from overweighting hundreds of securities that are too cheap without having to identify which securities are mispriced. In the short to intermediate term, however, fundamental indexing can trail capitalization-weighted strategies, particularly in markets where the biggest of the big companies are leading the market upward.

HOW TO ALLOCATE ASSETS IN YOUR PORTFOLIO

A diversified portfolio consists of a variety of asset categories that contain hundreds, if not thousands, of individual securities. It can include publicly traded securities and private holdings, such as rental real estate, that are not tied to the financial markets. It can include investments with a positive expected return that generate income and speculations such as gold or antiques with no income and whose success depends on others paying more for the asset in the future. Given the myriad of investment opportunities, both public and private, it just isn't practical to use a traditional asset allocation model based on modern portfolio theory to select an optimal portfolio. That requires too many assumptions, many of which are mere guesses.

Instead of using a complicated asset allocation model, you can choose an appropriate split between stocks and cash based on their expected returns and the financial harm a major decline in stocks would have on your lifestyle. Once that asset allocation foundation is in place, you can complement it with additional asset categories you have analyzed using our ten-question framework. The idea is to treat asset allocation less like an optimization problem and more like a creative endeavor where there are rules of thumb but no right answers. The key to is to be flexible and to lower the emotional stakes by making incremental changes as your knowledge of investing grows and your skill at analyzing investment opportunities increases.

AN ALTERNATIVE APPROACH

Some investors might not like the flexibility of making incremental changes and prefer to simplify their investing by choosing a target asset allocation and forgetting about it, other than to periodically rebalance to the target. They just want an asset garden with a few asset categories. One intriguing approach is to combine asset classes that perform differently under different economic regimes. For example, stocks perform well during periods when the economy is growing; on the other hand, bonds tend to do better when economic growth is slowing or contracting since interest rates usually decline during those periods, pushing up bond prices. Inflation-hedged bonds perform well during periods of high inflation, and commodities futures and gold tend to jump in price during periods of unexpected inflation. Falling inflation is a good environment for stocks and bonds.

A number of investment practitioners, such as Ray Dalio of Bridgewater Associates, have proposed portfolios containing asset categories that have historically done well during different economic environments.[14] These portfolios go by names like the All Seasons Portfolio, the Permanent Portfolio, and the Golden Butterfly. They often include allocations to long-term bonds, commodities, and gold, asset categories that can be as risky as stocks in terms of volatility and maximum drawdowns. Allocating a significant amount of capital to volatile asset categories besides stocks means the portfolio's return and volatility are no longer primarily driven by stocks.

For example, the degree to which a portfolio that is allocated 50% to stocks and 50% to cash deviates from its expected return is almost entirely driven by how stocks perform. Because cash will have a narrow range of returns in contrast to stocks, which could gain or lose 40% in a year, the portfolio outcome is highly correlated to the stock market even though it is 50% in cash. In contrast, a portfolio that is evenly divided between long-term bonds and stocks will have deviations from its expected returns determined by what happens to both the stock and bond markets, as long-term bonds can gain or fall 20% in a year. This, of course, is how diversification is supposed to work, with an asset category that performs quite poorly being offset by the strong performance of another asset category that does well. Yet this approach takes fortitude, as it requires an investor to stomach significant volatility in the individual portfolio components. A great resource to analyze the historical performance and risk of these role-based portfolios is Portfolios Charts at https://portfoliocharts.com/.[15] Of course, investors pursuing this approach need to recognize that although the portfolios have done well historically, that does not mean they will necessarily do so in the future. Starting conditions matter, particularly the yield to maturity/yield to worst of long-term bonds and Treasury Inflation-Protected Securities. A role-based portfolio is more likely to be successful when yields are higher than average than when they are near the low end of their historical range.

CHAPTER SUMMARY

- Choosing an asset allocation based on modern portfolio theory can give investors a false sense of confidence regarding portfolio outcomes.

- Rather than focus on the average expected return, individuals should make portfolio decisions based on the financial harm that extreme events such as a major stock market decline would have on their lifestyle.

- Individual investors should approach asset allocation not as an attempt to select a correct or optimal portfolio, but as a creative endeavor where there are rules of thumb but no right answers.

- With stocks and cash as the base layer, individuals can increase diversification by incrementally adding asset categories with different return drivers including opportunities that are public and private, domestic and international, capitalization weighted and fundamentally weighted.

- A simple asset allocation approach is to combine several highly volatile asset classes that do well under different economic environments, but the approach requires fortitude due to the potential wild swings in the individual components.

10

Should You Invest?

Applying the Investment Framework

THE TEN QUESTIONS

1. What is it?

2. Is it investing, speculating, or gambling?

3. What is the upside?

4. What is the downside?

5. Who is on the other side of the trade?

6. What is the investment vehicle?

7. What does it take to be successful?

8. Who is getting a cut?

9. How does it impact your portfolio?

10. **Should you invest?**

QUESTION TEN: SHOULD YOU INVEST?

Once we have identified an attractive investment opportunity, we have to decide when and how much to invest. How much to invest is a function of our confidence that an investment will be successful, the reliability of the return drivers for that success, and the personal financial harm caused if the investment falls short of our expectations. When to invest is a function of the amount of money we are seeking to put to work and current market conditions.

Now that we have covered the first nine investment questions, it is possible you are asking, "What do I do now? Where should I invest?" I am hopeful that by following the investing filters derived from the first nine questions, you have narrowed the universe of potential investments down considerably. That what *not* to do has become clearer. That you will avoid investments where a successful outcome is dependent on being precisely right about the future. That you will be hesitant to invest where the fees are too high, where success depends on outsmarting better-informed market participants, or when the investment is a zero-sum game in that for every winner there is a loser.

I am also hopeful you have greater clarity about what to do. That you have some additional tools to answer, "What is it?" That you are better able to understand the math and emotion of investing. The math is cash flow such as dividends, interest, and rent and how that cash flow grows over time as earnings or rent increases. The emotion is how investors are valuing investment cash flows. Are they paying a higher-than-average price for those cash flows, bidding up security prices, which means subsequent returns will likely be lower? Or are investors fearful and placing a low value on an investment's expected cash flow, suggesting subsequent returns could be higher?

An investment's expected upside, including its ability to exceed the rate of inflation, should be considered relative to its downside. What is the potential loss in terms of the maximum drawdown, and what would be the personal harm caused by the loss given the size of the investment you are considering? Where does the investment fit in the context of your overall investment portfolio? Does it provide additional diversification or variety in terms of the return driver? Do you understand the investment vehicle, its liquidity, and the fees? Are you clear about what has to happen for the investment to succeed?

We will never be certain our assumptions for an investment's return are correct. The outcome will likely differ from our estimate. Just as the black Claude mirrors attached to the window frames of the Grand Canyon's Desert View Watchtower made it easier for artists to frame a scene and compare different shades and colors, the discipline of deriving reasonable return assumptions and understanding the risk helps us compare one investment opportunity with another. Ultimately, after conducting your due diligence on an investment opportunity, you must answer the tenth question: "Should I invest?" If the answer is yes, then we need to decide when and how much.

As an institutional portfolio manager when our team decided to make a portfolio change by investing in a new security and selling all or a portion of an existing holding, I wanted to implement the change right away. I found it frustrating to have to wait several days to implement the decision, because we had to allocate the trade across so many client accounts. I wanted to immediately implement the change, because I felt like I had done the analysis, and I didn't want to miss out on the potential portfolio gains from the work I had done. As an individual, you can make a portfolio change right away. Yet the reality is making a portfolio change today or a few days from now is unlikely to impact your long-term performance. There is too much day-to-day randomness in markets for the timing to make that much of a difference, particularly for smaller trades.

DOLLAR-COST AVERAGING

The timing decision becomes more important when we receive a large lump sum from an inheritance, bonus, or buyout. As an investment advisor, I worked with not-for-profits that occasionally received large gifts that became a meaningful percentage of the institution's assets. The members of the boards of these institutions had to decide what to do with the money. Should they invest it all at once, or should they average into the market over a period of time? This second approach is called dollar-cost averaging. I shared with these board members historical studies that indicated investing the lump sum immediately was superior to dollar-cost averaging. The logic was simple. The stock market appreciates over time, so investing the lump sum immediately will statistically do better over most periods than averaging in, because the dollar-cost averaging approach will miss out on some of the early months of stock appreciation. Of course, if the stock market trends down in the early months of the investment, then dollar-cost averaging will perform better than investing the gift all at once.

Usually, the board members would dutifully look at the studies, acknowledge what the statistics said, and then choose to dollar-cost average. Why? They feared having to answer to the donor if the stock market plummeted shortly after investing the gift. They believed that would look imprudent. These board members could more easily envision the donor upset about the gift falling in value by 20% shortly after it was donated than they could envision the donor upset because the gift didn't appreciate as much using dollar-cost averaging. The boards acted to minimize their and the donor's maximum regret.

When we receive a large addition to our portfolios, it can take time to get used to managing a larger sum of money. The dollar amounts are bigger, and it feels like there is more at stake, even if the new funds were an unexpected gift or inheritance. Dollar-cost averaging can help ease the transition. The emotional benefit of dollar-cost averaging often trumps the rational analysis that says investing the new funds in one lump sum is statistically the better-performing option.

POSITION SIZE

When you decide to make a new investment, what should the position size be as a percentage of your portfolio? There isn't a right answer when it comes to position size. For a global ETF or index fund that holds thousands of underlying securities and whose success depends on the overall growth of the global economy, investors might be comfortable having their entire stock allocation invested in it. That is because the security represents a broad segment of the market. For more concentrated holdings, where success is dependent on idiosyncratic factors such as whether a closed-end fund's discount to net asset value narrows, investors may want to initially invest less than 2% of their portfolios in order to allow time to better understand the given security. I recall an investment manager that initially took 0.5% positions in stocks he was researching in order to keep the stocks on the radar and better understand how the securities traded. Position size is a function of our confidence that an investment will be successful, the reliability of the return drivers for that success, and the personal financial harm caused if the investment falls short of our expectations.

MARKET TIMING VERSUS RISK MANAGEMENT

As an investment manager and in my own portfolio, I have been comfortable adjusting my asset allocation based on market conditions. This is sometimes labeled as market timing and immediately dismissed by some as reckless and a strategy that rarely works. I agree that making large portfolio shifts from stocks to cash and back can be dangerous. That is not how I invest. During the great financial crisis of 2008, I was hired by a foundation where the board had panicked and sold much of the foundation's stock portfolio in late 2008. I began working with this foundation shortly after the board made this ill-timed decision. By then, the portfolio had already taken the brunt of portfolio losses. The board sold near the market bottom. In mid-2009 by the time we were able to come to an agreement on moving back into stocks, the stock market was well on its way to recovery.

Large market timing bets consist of two decisions: shifting (1) from stocks to cash and (2) from cash back to stocks. An investor who is correct 70% of the time on each of those individual decisions will statistically be correct on both decisions on a combined basis less than half of the time. Rather than make large portfolio shifts, I make incremental changes, rarely moving 5% to 10% of my portfolio at one time. At my former investment firm, we labeled this approach active asset allocation. Why should you bother making changes at all? Why not just stick to a target and rebalance on a periodic basis? That is certainly a valid approach—one we used for many of our institutional clients where we had a consulting relationship and didn't have the authority to make portfolio changes. I covered rebalancing in Chapter 8.

Yet if you are like me and don't have a set portfolio target, then a more opportunistic approach to asset allocation makes sense. This is the asset garden methodology I discussed in the previous chapter. The question to ask is, given the opportunity set of investments in terms of their expected returns, risks, and your level of understanding, do you have the appropriate portfolio mix? Do you own investments where you are no longer being adequately compensated for the risk, so it might be prudent to reduce exposure? Perhaps it is an area of the stock market such as small-company stocks or emerging markets stocks that have recorded extremely strong performance and are now selling for above-average valuations. Maybe it is a closed-end bond fund whose discount is now narrower than its historical average discount. Perhaps it is a high-yield bond fund where the spread or incremental yield relative to ten-year Treasuries has narrowed to below its long-term average spread of 5%. Alternatively, are there asset categories that have fallen in price and are now selling for valuations significantly below their historical averages?

I'll admit that one of the challenges with this approach is getting valuation metrics in order to compare an asset class's current valuation relative to its history. Many of the data providers charge thousands of dollars a year for this information. That is one reason I run a membership community in conjunction with my podcast, so I can provide members with timely valuation information to make more informed asset allocation decisions. Still, sufficient information is available in the financial press and can be gained, as well, by observing what is going on around us to identify risks and opportunities. It was clear that risks were high during the dot-com bubble in 1999 and 2000 and the cryptocurrency mania of 2017, given how prices of dot-com stocks and Bitcoin had soared and also how individuals who had previously taken little interest in investing were buying technology stocks and cryptocurrencies. Likewise, in 2009 there were numerous asset classes that were selling at some of their most attractive valuations in decades.

It is tempting before selling an asset that has appreciated to try to determine the market top. Likewise, it would be advantageous before buying to determine whether a bottom has been reached after an asset has plummeted in value. Timing the absolute top or bottom is difficult if not impossible to do. That is why an incremental approach works best. We can reduce exposure in small chunks as an asset class appreciates in price and becomes more expensive. We can add exposure when an asset class is attractively priced after a large sell-off. Sometimes it is helpful to wait for an asset class that has sold off to reverse course and begin to recover, but even then, it is possible the asset class might fall further. The reality is, you will be early. You will make mistakes. Sometimes the asset class will continue to fall after you bought it or rise after you sold. That's okay. Those kinds of mistakes are normal, if they can even be considered mistakes. The good news is, in the long run your portfolio performance will be better as you consistently buy asset classes that are less expensive than average and reduce exposure to asset classes that are more expensive than average. It is a buy-low, sell-high discipline. We cannot control the outcome of each of our investment decisions. What we can control is our decision-making process.

During the great financial crisis, I felt bad after we increased our clients' exposure to emerging markets stocks in the fall of 2008. We were three weeks too early, so our clients suffered additional losses. Yet the price-to-earnings ratio for emerging markets stocks was less than 10, one of their cheapest valuations ever. We didn't know exactly when the sell-off would end, but given the low valuations, the expected return for emerging markets was quite high and justified the risk. Our clients were rewarded even though we were early.

ECONOMIC TRENDS

While we can monitor the performance and valuations of our individual holdings, it is also prudent to be aware of economic trends, as they also impact our portfolio returns. Since 1916, ten of the twelve deepest drawdowns for U.S. stocks have occurred during economic recessions, with an average decline of 46%.[1] One way I monitor recession risk is by analyzing monthly manufacturing purchasing manager surveys, also known as PMI (Purchasing Managers' Index) surveys. These are surveys of manufacturing businesses conducted around the world by research firms such as IHS Markit and the Institute of Supply Management.[2] The companies that participate in these surveys are asked numerous questions on the state of their businesses, such as new orders, inventories, hiring plans, and pricing. There are also nonmanufacturing PMI surveys, but I focus on the manufacturing survey because it has a longer history and manufacturers are more sensitive to changes in the economy. When a country's manufacturing PMI is greater than 50, it is indicative of an economy that is expanding. When the PMI is less than 50, it is indicative of an economy that is slowing or contracting. When the PMI is less than 48, recession risk is high. For example, every U.S. recession since 1948 has seen a manufacturing PMI fall below 48. The last false positive when the U.S. PMI fell below 48 and there was no recession was in 1967.[3] As portfolio managers, when the economy is weakening as indicated by PMI, we have to decide whether we want to reduce risk by lowering our exposure to stocks, non-investment-grade bonds, and other risk assets or stay fully invested. The answer depends on the personal financial harm a 45%-or-more decline would cause. For many, who have decades until they retire, the financial harm could be minimal, so they can ride out the storm. For others, it may be prudent to incrementally reduce exposure to stocks as recession risks increase.

SOCIALLY RESPONSIBLE INVESTING

A final consideration when making a decision about a new investment is whether it aligns with our personal values. Making investment decisions based on moral or ethical values is known as socially responsible investing. Investors who seek to construct socially responsible portfolios often rely on environmental, social, and governance (ESG) data that measure how a company conducts business with regard to its policies and actions related to the environment, its employees, and the communities in which it operates.[4]

As an investment advisor, I had a number of environmental and religious organizations as clients who had ethical issues with investing in the stock or bonds of companies that generated profits in ways that violated these organizations' moral beliefs or mission. For larger portfolio allocations, we retained investment managers who could structure a portfolio that avoided holding so-called sin stocks that were inconsistent with the organizations' investment policies. For allocations that were smaller, such as allocations to emerging markets or U.S. small-capitalization stocks, the clients often didn't have sufficient assets to meet the account minimums of separate account managers in those areas. In those situations, we utilized mutual funds, index funds, or exchange-traded funds.

These organizations had to balance their unwillingness to invest in certain untenable securities with their desire to generate the best possible portfolio return in a diversified manner. They needed to answer the following: Is it better to achieve a higher portfolio return that allows an organization to do more good in fulfilling its social mission while worrying less about whether the portfolio's securities are aligned with that mission? Or is it better to accept a lower portfolio return that is generated in a more environmentally or socially responsible manner, but in turn leaves fewer resources for the organization to do good? Ideally, an organization or an individual wouldn't need to make that trade-off if socially responsible portfolios outperformed the overall stock market.

Unfortunately, that is difficult to determine. Performance differentials (both outperformance and underperformance) between a socially responsible investment fund and the overall market may be due to factors that have nothing to do with the ESG screens utilized. For example, a socially responsible portfolio might have a smaller average market capitalization relative to the market, and if smaller companies outperform larger companies over the measured period, then the socially responsible portfolio will also outperform the market.

In addition, if shareholders divest from companies that violate their moral values, yet customers continue to purchase the companies' products and services, then the stocks of the questionable companies may actually outperform the overall market. That's because lower demand for the controversial stocks could result in lower valuations and thus higher dividend yields. If the companies continue to register solid sales and earnings growth, then the controversial stocks will outperform their more socially responsible competitors due to the higher dividend yield. Consequently, an important way consumers can impact the stock performance of companies that don't meet their environmental, social, and governance standards is to stop buying the companies' products or services and encourage others to stop buying. If a large enough group boycotts the particular product or service, it will impact those companies' revenues, earnings, and ultimately their stock price.

In January 2018, Laurence Fink, chief executive of BlackRock, the world's largest asset manager, sent a letter to the CEOs of companies BlackRock owns to say that it is no longer enough to deliver excellent financial performance. Fink wrote: "To prosper over time, every company must not only deliver financial performance, but also show how it makes a positive contribution to society. Companies must benefit all of their stakeholders, including shareholders, employees, customers, and the communities in which they operate."[5]

Umair Haque labels companies that generate profits by simply exceeding their financial cost of capital as creating "thin value." Recall from Chapter 5 that a firm's cost of capital reflects investors' return expectations for the company's stock and bonds. Historically, if a business continually executes on projects that exceed the cost of capital, then the market valuation as reflected in the company's stock price increases. Fink and Haque suggest that seeking to increase shareholder value by pursuing initiatives that exceed the cost of capital is too narrow a focus. Thin value might look good on a financial statement, but it may have been achieved by shifting environmental and social costs to nonstakeholders. Instead, companies should create what Haque calls "thick value." Thick value is created when companies exceed their cost of capital and "generate profits by activities whose benefits accrue sustainably, authentically, and meaningfully to people, communities, society, the natural world, and future generations."[6]

PIECEMEAL PORTFOLIO MANAGERS

We have seen in this chapter that once you have identified an attractive investment opportunity, there are some additional considerations such as, does the investment meet your values, how much should you invest, and when should you invest? These are never clear-cut decisions. All we can do is use our best judgment. Philosopher Karl Popper advocates the concept of the piecemeal engineer, which is how I like to approach investment management. A piecemeal engineer does not believe in "re-designing . . . as a whole,"[7] which in a portfolio context means we don't make huge portfolio changes all at once. Instead, a piecemeal engineer makes "small adjustments and readjustments which can be continually improved upon. . . . The piecemeal engineer knows, like Socrates, how little he knows. He knows that we can learn only from our mistakes. Accordingly, he will make his way, step by step, carefully comparing the results expected with the results achieved, and always on the look-out for the unavoidable, unwanted consequences of any reform."[8] Applying this approach as piecemeal portfolio managers will allow us to incrementally become better investors as we make small changes and learn what we can from the outcomes.

CHAPTER SUMMARY

- Successful investing is as much about what *not* to do as it is about what to do.

- The emotional benefit of dollar-cost averaging often trumps the rational analysis that says investing the new funds in one lump sum is statistically the better-performing option.

- Position size is a function of our confidence that an investment will be successful, the reliability of the return drivers for that success, and the personal financial harm caused if the investment falls short of our expectations.

- Portfolio performance will be better as we incrementally adjust our portfolios by consistently buying asset classes that are less expensive and reducing exposure to asset classes that are more expensive. It is a buy-low, sell-high discipline.

- PMI data is helpful for monitoring economic trends that can impact our portfolio performance.

- Consumers can impact the stock performance of companies that don't meet their environmental, social, and governance standards by not buying and encouraging others not to buy the companies' products or services. If a large enough group boycotts the particular product or service, it will impact those companies' revenues, earnings, and ultimately their stock price.

Conclusion

If you have made it this far in the book, you are now more familiar with the tools and the knowledge you need to master successful investing. My hope is that you also have a greater sense of confidence as you allocate capital to cash flow–generating investments. You don't need to be an expert to be a successful investor. You need a disciplined investment process, a framework you can adhere to that provides peace of mind when others panic. The smartest and most successful investors I know have no more idea about what is going to happen in the future than you do. Instead, they have an investment philosophy and discipline that guides their investment choices. They also have the wisdom that comes from making investment decisions in the face of extreme uncertainty. Sometimes those decisions work out well. At other times the decisions lead to undesirable outcomes even when the investment managers follow a good decision-making process. Sometimes the managers are just wrong and miss something in their analysis.

As I shared in Chapter 3, I gained needed experience in the aftermath of recommending a university endowment client invest in high-yield bonds in the late 1990s after a period of strong performance. I learned that historical performance is a lousy basis for making an investment decision. I viscerally felt that mistake each time I met with that client and reviewed the high-yield bond manager performance. I learned I needed to better understand what drives the return of a given investment. Doing so and analyzing current conditions allows us to develop a reasonable return assumption. That was the approach I took in late 2008 when I again recommended high-yield bonds to clients at a time when other investors were fleeing the asset class. I didn't know if the bottom was in place, but I knew with the yield to maturity for high-yield bonds close to 20%, that my clients could do very well in the coming years with that investment. And they did.

When I began my career as an investment advisor, I was convinced there were investment managers and strategists who could accurately forecast what was going to happen. Managers that had things figured out. I spent years researching stock and bond managers, hedge funds, and other investment advisory firms to identify those managers who appeared to be the most skilled. Those who had some type of informational edge that allowed them to accurately predict what was likely to happen and profit from it. I never found any people with that level of successful forecasting ability. They don't exist.

The most successful investors I know are asset allocators and risk managers. They survey the investment universe and allocate capital to areas that they believe are most likely to have an asymmetric risk-reward trade-off in that the upside potential is significantly greater than the potential losses. The investor with this approach from whom I have learned the most is Seth Klarman, founder of the investment partnership the Baupost Group. His firm manages a significant percentage of one of my former advisory client's assets. He is considered one of the most successful investors of all time.[1] For a number of years, I met annually with Klarman at his firm's offices to discuss his investment philosophy and process. I read and reread his annual client letters going back to 1983. Klarman says that successful investors have "the arrogance to act, and act decisively, and the humility to know that you could be wrong. The acuity, flexibility, and willingness to change your mind when you realize you are wrong, and the stubbornness to refuse to do so when you remain justifiably confident in your thesis. . . . The integrity to admit mistakes, the fortitude to risk making more of them, and the intellectual honesty not to confuse luck with skill."[2]

Throughout this book, I have reiterated that as individuals we are portfolio managers and risk managers. Our charge as we oversee our personal assets is to actively allocate to the areas of the market that are most compelling in terms of the expected return and valuation and avoid areas where investors are overly optimistic, suggesting future returns will be lower. Portfolio management is not about accurately predicting the future or outsmarting other investors. It is the process of combining multiple asset categories that contribute to a positive return that earns more than the rate of inflation while minimizing the personal financial harm caused by major market drawdowns. Portfolio management is about understanding the math and emotion of investing and recognizing there isn't a right answer, a perfectly optimized portfolio, just as there aren't optimized flower or vegetable gardens.

Each morning upon waking, we evaluate the weather and decide what to wear. Choosing an outfit is not an optimization problem. Andrew W. Lo points out that he can create over 2 million unique outfits from his wardrobe consisting of 10 shirts, 10 pairs of pants, 5 jackets, 20 ties, 10 pairs of socks, and 4 pairs of shoes. If he spent one second considering each possible outfit, it would take him nearly 24 days to make a decision. Our decision about what to wear is a satisficing problem. Satisfice is a word coined by economist Herbert Alexander Simon. It is a combination of *satisfy* and *suffice*.[3] When we satisfice, we seek to make a good enough decision, not an optimal one. We dress based on weather conditions, using rules of thumb derived from what has worked in the past—from positive and negative feedback. Outfits that receive compliments from others we wear again and again, while we no longer wear outfits we feel make us look silly. Of course, not everyone dresses the same way. Some prefer to dress more minimalist, perhaps wearing a basic uniform each day. Others prefer more complexity in their dress with multiple layers, scarves, and accessories. Some are in tune with current trends and seek to be on the cutting edge of fashion. And then there are those who outsource wardrobe selection to a stylist.

Investing is similar. We consider longer-term return expectations as well as risk. We monitor current investment conditions such as how expensive or cheap stocks are or what yield can we get on bonds. Then we select a portfolio based on those expectations in the same way we select a wardrobe. We satisfice, making good enough choices derived from our experience. Not everyone's portfolio will be the same. There will be customization based on individual preferences. Some will want a minimalist portfolio with only two or three holdings. Others prefer to fine-tune their strategy with multiple asset classes. Some will chase after the latest investment fad. And others will outsource their investment selection to an investment advisor in the same way a celebrity might depend on a stylist.

No matter your personal investment style, answering these ten questions will help you make better investment decisions:

1. **WHAT IS IT?** We should seek to understand and explain in simple terms an investment's characteristics. The act of explaining keeps us humble and helps us realize what we don't know.

2. **IS IT INVESTING, SPECULATION, OR GAMBLING?** Classifying financial opportunities by whether they have a greater likelihood to be profitable, to be unprofitable, or to have an outcome that is highly uncertain simplifies the investing universe. Our research time is reduced when we focus most of our efforts on financial opportunities that have a positive expected return.

3. **WHAT IS THE UPSIDE?** We can use rules of thumb to estimate an investment's expected return. This allows us to compare

different opportunities and make sure our assumptions are reasonable.

4. **WHAT IS THE DOWNSIDE?** The downside of an investment consists of its maximum potential loss and the personal financial harm caused by that loss. When evaluating an investment's downside, the goal is to avoid irreparable financial harm rather than to avoid any loss at all. If you rule out any possibility of a loss in your investing, then you are probably reducing risk too much, and your portfolio might not keep pace with inflation.

5. **WHO IS ON THE OTHER SIDE OF THE TRADE?** Knowing who is selling us an investment helps us avoid financial instruments where success is dependent on knowing the future and/or outsmarting other investors.

6. **WHAT IS THE INVESTMENT VEHICLE?** An investment vehicle is an instrument, product, or container that houses a particular investment strategy. Before investing, we should be able to explain an investment vehicle's attributes including the expected return, the risk in terms of the potential maximum drawdown, liquidity, fees, structure, and pricing.

7. **WHAT DOES IT TAKE TO BE SUCCESSFUL?** All investments have return drivers, such as income, cash flow growth, leverage, and other attributes that determine their performance. Successful portfolios have a diversified mix of dependable return drivers that we have identified beforehand.

8. **WHO IS GETTING A CUT?** Successful investors are aware of the entities taking a portion of the return in the form of fees, expenses, and taxes. We should make sure we receive sufficient benefits for any fees we pay.

9. **HOW DOES IT IMPACT YOUR PORTFOLIO?** We shouldn't approach asset allocation as an optimization problem with a single right answer. Rather, using guidelines and

rules of thumb, we have tremendous creative freedom to build diversified investment portfolios that align with our knowledge, interests, and values.

10. **SHOULD YOU INVEST?** Once we have identified an attractive investment opportunity, we have to decide when and how much to invest. How much to invest is a function of our confidence that an investment will be successful, the reliability of the return drivers for that success, and the personal financial harm caused if the investment falls short of our expectations. When to invest is a function of how much money we are seeking to put to work and current market conditions.

In our investment selection process, it is helpful to have some guides, including virtual mentors and model portfolios. I am hopeful this book can serve as an additional guide in your role as a portfolio manager. If it has and you think it would be helpful to others you know, I would be honored if you would share it with them. Thank you for reading.

Glossary of Terms

Active asset allocation: The process of making incremental changes to a portfolio based on market conditions such as valuations or economic trends.

Active management: An investment process in which investment managers seek to outperform a target index or benchmark by structuring a portfolio that differs from the benchmark.

Active managers: Investment managers who pursue active management strategies.

Administrative fees: Fees that compensate brokerage firms, fund companies, and retirement plan administrators for tracking investments, preparing and sending out statements and tax documents, and conducting other administrative tasks related to client account management.

Advisory/management fees: Funds paid to investment professionals to manage specific investment vehicles or client portfolios.

Annualized return: The rate of return an investor has earned on an annual basis. It is calculated by taking the cumulative return earned over the entire holding period and scaling it to a one-year time period.

Ask price: The current offer price if an investor wants to buy shares of a particular security.

Asset: A financial security, property, or item of value that can be sold and converted to cash.

Asset allocation: The process of dividing up a portfolio into different asset classes.

Asset category: A less formal name for an asset class.

Asset class: A basket or group of securities with similar characteristics.

Authorized participants: Institutional traders that work with exchange-traded fund (ETF) sponsors to create and redeem ETF shares in large trading blocks.

Autocallable note: An investment security that can be redeemed early by the sponsor if certain conditions are met such as reaching a particular price target.

Bid price: The current offer price if an investor wants to sell shares of a particular security.

Binary option: A security with a binary payoff, usually $100 or $0, where an investor pays a premium to place a bet on whether the underlying asset that the option contract is based on will increase or decrease in value.

Bitcoin: One of the original and largest cryptocurrencies in terms of the value outstanding.

Bond duration: A mathematical estimate of a bond's or a bond portfolio's price sensitivity to changing interest rates.

Bond managers: Investment professionals who manage a portfolio of bonds for clients.

Bond maturity: The date upon which a bond issuer redeems a bond by paying off the principal balance.

Bonds: Debt instruments issued by governments, corporations, and other entities to raise money for new projects or ongoing operations. Investors purchase new bond issues for the principal amount, and the issuer pays investors interest on the debt and returns the principal when the bond matures, unless the bond issuer defaults.

Broker: An individual that acts as an intermediary to facilitate the buying and selling of assets.

Brokerage firm: An entity that facilitates the trading of investment securities by acting as an intermediary between buyers and sellers.

Broad-based ETF: An exchange-traded fund with hundreds or thousands of underlying holdings that seeks to replicate the performance of a large segment of the financial markets such as global stocks or U.S. stocks.

Capital: The financial assets owned by an individual, household, or business.

Capital gain distribution: A taxable payment to the shareholders of a mutual fund or ETF that represents the realized profits from the manager selling the fund's or ETF's underlying holdings.

Capital markets: The financial markets involving the sale and trading of investment securities such as stocks and bonds so that businesses can raise funds for their ongoing operations or new initiatives.

Capitalization rate: A key metric in evaluating real estate that is calculated by dividing a project's net operating income by its costs or market value.

Capitalization weighted: A method of constructing a market index or benchmark in which the underlying holdings are weighted by size as reflected in a holding's price and the number of shares outstanding.

Cash: Money either held physically in the form of bills and coins or held at a financial institution in an account that is easily accessible.

Cash equivalents: Very short term investment securities such as U.S. Treasury bills that can easily be sold and converted to cash.

Cash flow: Cash generated by an underlying investment usually in the form of interest, dividends, or rents that is distributed to the asset owner.

Cash flow growth: The rate at which an income stream increases over time.

Certificate of deposit: An insured financial product issued by banks, credit unions, and other financial institutions that pays a specified rate of interest over a designated term.

Change in valuation: How the price of an asset changes based on what investors are willing to pay for current and anticipated future cash flows.

Close: To end a particular security trade, usually by selling it or by taking an opposing position.

Closed-end fund: A registered commingled fund with a fixed amount of shares that trades on an exchange and is overseen by a professional investment manager.

Collateral: Assets pledged as security to be sold in case a borrower defaults on a loan or other debt instrument.

Commingled fund: A professionally managed investment vehicle that pools money from investors and buys and sells investment securities.

Commodities: Raw materials such as agricultural products (e.g., wheat, corn), metals (e.g., copper, gold), and energy sources (e.g., oil, natural gas).

Commodity futures: Contractual agreements to buy or sell a specific commodity on a future date.

Common stock: An investment security that represents ownership in a company and entitles the holder to a share of the profits in the form of a dividend.

Complex adaptive system: A system composed of a wide variety of interconnected inputs that adapt and learn over time so that the behavior of the system cannot be accurately predicted by studying the individual parts.

Consumer price index (CPI): An inflation measure that tracks the average price change for a reference basket of goods and services.

Cost basis: The original value of an asset for calculating taxes.

Cost of capital: The rate of return that serves as the minimum threshold or hurdle rate for a company to pursue a new project or initiative. The cost of capital is calculated by taking the weighted average of the interest rate on a company's debt and the estimated return requirement for stock investors.

Counterparty: The entity on the other side of a financial transaction that is acting as the buyer or seller.

Counterparty risk: The risk that the entity on the other side of a financial transaction defaults on its contractual obligations.

Creation basket: The reference basket of securities that an ETF sponsor will accept in exchange for newly issued ETF shares.

Cryptocurrency: A digital asset designed to facilitate financial transactions between parties in a secure and decentralized fashion.

Default: The failure of an entity to perform its contractual obligation such as the payment of interest or return of principal.

Defined benefit plan: A retirement plan in which the employer promises specific retirement benefits that are tied to an employee's age, earnings, and tenure.

Defined contribution plan: A retirement plan in which employees and employers make contributions and whose value depends on the return of the financial markets.

Derivative contract: A financial agreement whose value is determined by the price of an agreed-upon financial asset.

Dip: A temporary setback in the price of a security before it continues to increase.

Distressed debt investing: A strategy of buying the debt of a company that is in or near bankruptcy in order to profit from the company's eventual restructuring.

Distribution yield: The measure of the cash flow paid by a mutual fund or exchange-traded fund as a percentage of its net asset value. The distribution yield is typically calculated by annualizing the most recent monthly or quarterly distribution.

Diversification: The strategy of combining a variety of investments with different return drivers into a portfolio.

Dividend: The cash flow paid by a company or fund to its shareholders.

Dividend investing: A strategy of investing in securities with high dividend yields.

Dividend yield: A measure of an investment's dividend rate calculated by annualizing the most recent monthly or quarterly dividend and dividing it by the security's price.

Dollar-cost average: The practice of investing a set amount of cash at regular intervals.

Dot-com bubble: The period in the late 1990s to early 2000s denoted by the rapid increase in the price and valuations of technology stocks due to excessive zeal regarding the expanding use of the internet.

Downside: An investment's maximum potential loss and the personal financial harm caused by that loss.

Economic growth: The rate at which a country's gross domestic product changes from one period to the next.

Efficient frontier: A line graph composed of optimal portfolios with the highest expected return for a given level of expected volatility.

Efficient market: A financial market in which all securities are priced correctly in that they reflect the securities' intrinsic value.

Environmental, social, and governance (ESG) data: Metrics that indicate how a company conducts business in terms of its policies and actions related to the environment, its employees, and the communities in which it operates.

Equities: Common stock representing ownership in a company.

Exchange: A financial market in which investment securities are bought and sold.

Exchange-traded funds (ETFs): Marketable securities that trade on an exchange and seek to track a specific index or segment of the capital markets, such as large-company stocks, bonds, or REITs.

Factor: A broad, persistent driver of return such as low valuations, high dividend yields, or price momentum.

Fixed income: Investments in bonds.

Flash crash: Sudden and severe price dislocations in investment securities that can be caused by a lack of willing buyers.

Foreign exchange (forex): The largest financial market in the world in which currencies are traded.

Fundamental indexing: A method of constructing a market index or benchmark in which the underlying holdings are weighted not by size but by other metrics such as revenue, earnings, or dividend yield.

Futures: *See* commodity futures.

Gamble: An opportunity with a negative expected return and a greater likelihood of losing money.

Great financial crisis: The global financial crisis of 2007 to 2009 marked by a severe economic contraction and falling asset prices.

Gross domestic product (GDP): The monetary value of a nation's output in terms of the goods and services produced during a given period.

Growth stocks: Common stocks with above-average earnings growth.

Hedge: An investment strategy that protects against market losses or currency fluctuations by entering into transactions that offset those potential losses.

Hedge fund: A commingled investment partnership in which institutions and high-net-worth individuals invest and that is overseen by a professional money manager who pursues a variety of investment strategies in an attempt to generate a positive return with minimal losses.

Heuristic: A simplified rule of thumb for making a decision.

High-yield bonds: Bonds issued by riskier companies that have been deemed speculative by bond rating agencies due to their higher risk of default.

Illiquid asset: An investment security that cannot easily be sold and converted to cash.

Illiquidity premium: The additional return for investing in an illiquid asset.

Index fund: A mutual fund whose investment objective is to replicate the performance of a specific index or segment of the capital markets, such as large-company stocks, bonds, or REITs.

Inflation: The generalized rise in prices over time that leads to a loss of purchasing power.

Initial public offering (IPO): The process by which a private company raises capital by issuing common stock to the public for the first time.

Interest rate: The percentage of principal on an annual basis that a borrower pays for the use of someone's money.

Intraday liquidity: The ability to buy or sell a financial security throughout the trading day.

Intrinsic value: The correct price of an investment based on the present value of its future cash flow stream.

Investment: A financial opportunity that has a positive expected return, usually because it generates income or is expected to do so in the future.

Investment conditions: The current characteristics of a financial security or asset class such as the valuation, earnings growth, or yield.

Investment vehicle: An instrument, product, or container that houses a particular investment strategy.

Junk bonds: *See* High-yield bonds.

Leverage (levered): The use of borrowed money to magnify an investment's return.

Limit order: An order to buy or sell a financial security at a specified price.

Limit up–limit down rules: Stock exchange rules that halt the trading of specific securities after they exhibit large short-term price moves.

Liquidity: A measure of how quickly and easily an investment can be sold, what is the cost for doing so, and how long after selling an investor receives the money.

Load: The commission paid to buy or redeem shares in an open-end mutual fund.

Low cost basis: When a security has appreciated a great deal in price and therefore would have a large taxable gain if it were sold.

Lump sum: The receipt of a large single payment.

Macro inefficiency: A situation in which an asset class appears to separate from a reasonable valuation in terms of a bubble forming or the asset class becoming extremely inexpensive relative to its historical valuation.

Maintenance margin: The minimum account balance a broker requires when investing in commodities futures.

Margin loan: Loans made to investors by brokerage firms, usually for the investor to buy additional securities.

Market capitalization: The size of a publicly traded company calculated by multiplying its stock price by the number of stock shares outstanding.

Market timing: The practice of making large portfolio shifts, usually from stocks to cash and back again.

Math of investing: The mechanics of what drives the returns of a particular investment.

Maturity: *See* Bond maturity.

Maximum drawdown: An estimate of an investment's worst expected percentage decline usually based on its worst historical decline.

Micro efficiency: A situation in which active managers are unable to identify and profit from security mispricings.

Modern portfolio theory (MPT): A financial theory introduced by Harry Markowitz that posits there is an optimal portfolio mix (i.e., the split between stocks, bonds, real estate, and other asset classes) that maximizes the expected return for a given level of volatility.

Momentum investing: An investment strategy that consists of buying securities that exhibit an upward price trend under the assumption that the trend will continue.

Money market mutual fund: A type of open-end mutual fund that invests in cash equivalents.

Municipal bonds: Debt securities issued by states, local governments, and school districts to fund various projects such as roads, utility infrastructure, and schools. Most municipal bonds are exempt from federal taxes and in many cases state and local taxes.

Mutual fund: *See* Open-end mutual fund.

Net asset value (NAV): The value of a commingled investment vehicle such as a mutual fund, ETF, or closed-end fund that is calculated by taking the value of a financial vehicle's assets including cash, subtracting the liabilities, and dividing by the number of shares outstanding.

Net operating income: The income a real estate project earns after deducting operating expenses such as property management fees and taxes.

Nominal GDP: The non-inflation-adjusted monetary value of a nation's output in terms of the goods and services produced during a given period. Usually, GDP is reported on a real basis in order to compare economic output from one period with output from a different period, net of the inflation impact.

Nominal price: The value of something in current dollars that has not been adjusted to factor in the impact of inflation.

Non-investment-grade bonds: *See* High-yield bonds.

Nonlinear system: A system in which the outcome is not proportional to the inputs and that frequently leads to different outcomes even when the inputs are similar.

Offering memorandum: The legal document that describes the details of a private investment offering such as the manager of the investment, the investment process, the fees, and the risks involved.

Open-end mutual fund: A registered commingled fund with an unlimited number of shares that is overseen by a professional investment manager. The price of an open-end mutual fund always equals the fund's net asset value.

Open position: A security trade that has yet to be closed.

Options: Investment securities that give an investor the right but not the obligation to purchase or sell an underlying investment at a certain price in the future.

Passive management: An investment process in which investment managers seek to replicate the performance of a target index or benchmark by structuring a portfolio that closely resembles the benchmark.

Pension plan: *See* Defined benefit plan.

Piecemeal portfolio manager: An investor who makes small, incremental portfolio changes rather than large, aggressive moves.

Portfolio: A collection of assets held by an individual or institution.

Portfolio management: The process of combining multiple asset categories that contribute to a positive real portfolio return while minimizing the financial harm caused by major market drawdowns.

Portfolio manager: An individual who compares different investment opportunities and allocates money among them.

Position size: The percentage of a portfolio allocated to a specific investment.

Present value: The value today of a future cash flow stream. Present value is calculated by reducing or discounting the future cash flow payments by a specific interest rate that usually equates to either the expected return on those future cash flow payments or the cost of capital.

Price-to-earnings (P/E) ratio: The price investors are willing to pay for a dollar's worth of earnings. It is calculated by dividing a stock's price by its historical or expected earnings.

Principal: The original amount of money that was lent or borrowed in a financial transaction.

Promissory note: A contractual agreement to pay interest and/or principal at a scheduled time or under certain conditions.

Prospectus: The legal document that describes the details of a public investment offering such as the manager of the investment, the investment process, the fees, and the risks involved.

Public offering: The process by which a private company raises capital by issuing common stock to the public.

Purchasing Managers' Index (PMI): A monthly survey of businesses on current and expected business conditions, such as new orders, inventory, hiring plans, and pricing, that is used as an economic indicator.

Real estate: Buildings and property that generate a rate of return through rental income and/or price appreciation.

Real estate crowdfunding: The practice of raising money from individuals via the internet to invest in real estate transactions.

Real estate investment trusts (REITs): Securities that own commercial real estate properties such as office buildings, apartments, storage units, hotels, and retail locations such as strip malls.

Real interest rate: The rate of interest after adjusting for the impact of inflation.

Real price: The value of something after it has been adjusted for the impact of inflation.

Real return: The expected or actual return on an investment after adjusting for the impact of inflation.

Real yield: The yield on a security that has been adjusted to reflect the impact of inflation. An example of a real yield is the yield on Treasury Inflation-Protected Securities.

Rebalancing: The act of selling one asset that has performed well and is overweight relative to a given target and allocating the proceeds to an asset that has not performed as well and is underweight relative to its target.

Recovery period: The time it takes for an investment to recoup its losses.

Return drivers: An investment's attributes, such as income, cash flow growth, or leverage, that determine its performance.

Satisfice: A word coined by economist Herbert Alexander Simon by combining *satisfy* and *suffice* and that means to make a good enough decision rather than an optimal one.

SEC yield: A standard yield calculation required by the U.S. Securities and Exchange Commission for bond funds and ETFs. The SEC yield is equivalent to a fund's yield to worst minus its operating expenses, such as the investment management fee charged by the mutual fund or ETF.

Secondary market: The financial markets in which previously issued investment securities are traded among buyers and sellers.

Securities lending: The practice of loaning securities for a fee in order to facilitate short selling.

Security: A tradable financial instrument in which an investor has an ownership right.

Senior debt: Debt that takes priority over other debt in terms of payment and access to collateral in the case of default.

Shareholders: The owners of an investment security such as a stock, ETF, or mutual fund.

Short selling: An investment technique that involves selling borrowed security shares in order to profit from the decline in a security's price.

Smart beta: An investment strategy that systematically seeks to harvest the return premium from tradable factors such as value, momentum, or high dividends.

Speculation: An opportunity where the investment outcome is highly uncertain and there is disagreement whether the return will be positive or negative.

Spot price: The current price at which an asset can be bought or sold.

Standard deviation: The statistical measure used to estimate volatility in asset allocation models based on modern portfolio theory. Standard deviation measures how spread out the data points are from the average value.

Stock: *See* Common stock.

Stock buyback: When a company buys its stock in the secondary market so that there are fewer shares outstanding.

Tax-deferred investment vehicle: An account, such as an individual retirement account (IRA) or 401(k) plan, that allows for income and realized gains to accumulate tax-free until distributions are taken from the account.

Tax liability: The amount of taxes owed to a government entity.

Term premium: The additional yield investors demand when investing in bonds as compensation for uncertainty regarding higher-than-expected inflation and future real rates of interest.

Tracking error: A measure of how the return of an actively managed investment portfolio or fund deviates from the return of its target benchmark.

Trading costs: Money in the form of a commission or a transaction fee that is paid to a broker or advisor to enter or exit an investment.

Trading halt: When a stock exchange temporarily suspends the trading of a security.

Treasuries: Bonds and other debt obligations issued by a federal government.

Treasury Inflation-Protected Securities (TIPS): Bonds issued by the U.S. government that are indexed to inflation in order to protect investors against rising prices.

Unhedged: A situation where an investment portfolio is not protected from market losses or currency fluctuations.

Unsecured: A liability in which there is no asset pledged as collateral in case of default.

Upside: The expected return of an investment opportunity.

Valuations: Financial metrics that indicate how a security or asset class is priced relative to its historical average or other securities.

Value investing: An investment style focused on buying stocks or other securities at a price below their intrinsic value.

Venture capital: Investments in privately owned start-up companies.

Volatility: How much a security or asset class deviates from its expected or average return.

Weighted average: A calculated average in which each observation used to calculate the average is multiplied by a specific weight such as its size. Weighted average differs from the simple average in which each observation is weighted equally in that the sum of all the observations is divided by the number of observations.

Weighted average maturity: The average amount of time until a portfolio of bonds matures calculated by taking the percentage allocated in each bond multiplied by the time until it matures in months or years.

Weighting: The percentage of a portfolio or index allocated to a specific security.

Yield to maturity: An estimate of a bond's or bond fund's total return if the bonds are held to maturity.

Yield to worst: An estimate of a bond's or bond fund's total return if the bonds are held to maturity or until they are redeemed early upon meeting certain conditions.

Zero-sum game: A game in which for every winner there is a loser.

Bibliography

2018 Investment Company Fact Book: A Review of Trends and Activities in the Investment Company Industry. 58th ed. Washington, DC: Investment Company Institute, 2018. Accessed October 4, 2018. https://www.ici .org/pdf/2018_factbook.pdf.

"Amazon.com, Inc. Revenue & Earnings per Share (EPS)." Nasdaq. Accessed March 28, 2019. https://www.nasdaq.com/symbol/amzn/ revenue-eps.

Anderson, Bendix. "Investment Sales Slowdown Hits the Student Housing Sector." *National Real Estate Investor.* July 17, 2017. Accessed October 18, 2018. https://www.nreionline.com/student-housing/ investment-sales-slowdown-hits-student-housing-sector.

Andrea. E-mail message to author. October 11–15, 2018.

Ang, Andrew. *Asset Management: A Systematic Approach to Factor Investing.* Oxford: Oxford University Press, 2014.

"Apple Inc. (AAPL) Stock Report." Nasdaq. Accessed November 8, 2018. https://www.nasdaq.com/symbol/aapl/stock-report.

Arnott, Rob, Noah Beck, Vitali Kalesnik, and John West. "How Can 'Smart Beta' Go Horribly Wrong?" Research Affiliates. February 2016.

Accessed October 17, 2018. https://www.researchaffiliates.com/en_us/ publications/articles/442_how_can_smart_beta_go_horribly_wrong .html.

Arnott, Rob, Shane Shepherd, and Bradford Cornell. "Yes. It's a Bubble. So What?" Research Affiliates. April 2018. Accessed October 19, 2018. https://www.researchaffiliates.com/en_us/publications/articles/668-yes -its-a-bubble-so-what.html.

Arnott, Rob, Vitali Kalesnik, and Lillian Wu. "The Incredible Shrinking Factor Return." Research Affiliates. April 2017. Accessed October 18, 2018. https://www.researchaffiliates.com/documents/601-The Incredible Shrinking Factor Return.pdf?mod=article_inline.

"Average Premium/Discount" widget. Closed-End Fund Association. Accessed October 5, 2018. http://www.cefa.com.

Bak, Per. "The Sandpile Paradigm." Chap. 3 in *How Nature Works: The Science of Self-Organized Criticality*. New York: Copernicus, 1996.

Ben-David, Itzhak, Francesco A. Franzoni, and Rabih Moussawi. "Do ETFs Increase Volatility?" Fisher College of Business Working Paper 2011-03-20, December 2, 2011. Last revised November 30, 2017. doi:10.2139/ssrn.1967599.

"Benefits of Binary Options." Nadex. April 10, 2018. https:// www.nadex.com/binary-options/benefits-of-binary-options.

Bernstein, Peter L. "What Happens If We're Wrong?" *New York Times*. June 22, 2008. Accessed September 19, 2018. https://www.nytimes .com/2008/06/22/business/22view.html?_r=1&oref=slogin&ref =business&pagewanted=print.

Bernstein, William J., and Robert D. Arnott. "Earnings Growth: The Two Percent Dilution." *Financial Analysts Journal* 59, no. 5 (September/ October 2003): 47–55. doi:10.2469/faj.v59.n5.2563.

"Capital Market Expectations Methodology Overview." Research Affiliates. Revised October 1, 2014. Accessed February 19, 2019.

https://www.researchaffiliates.com/documents/AA-Expected-Returns
-Methodology.pdf.

Chart B336B. Ned Davis Research. Accessed September 20, 2018.
https://www.ndr.com/ group/ndr/content-viewer/-/v/B336B.

Chart S09. Ned Davis Research. Accessed October 19, 2018. https://
www.ndr.com/group/ndr/content-viewer/-/v/S09.

Chart S1102. Ned Davis Research. Accessed September 20, 2018.
https://www.ndr.com/group/ndr/content-viewer/-/v/S1102.

Chart T_635.RPT. Ned Davis Research. Accessed September 25, 2018.
https://www.ndr.com/group/ndr/content-viewer/-/v/T_635*RPT.

Cicero, M. Tullius. *De Officiis*. Translated by Walter Miller. Cambridge,
MA: Harvard University Press, 1913. Accessed September 27, 2018.
http://www.perseus.tufts.edu/hopper/text?doc=Perseus:text:2007.01
.0048:book=pos=3:section=50.

"Closed-End Funds Daily Pricing." *CEF Connect*. Accessed October 5,
2018. https://www.cefconnect.com/closed-end-funds-daily-pricing.

Dalio, Ray. Introduction to *Principles: Life and Work*. New York: Simon
& Schuster, 2017. Kindle.

Davis, Ned. *Being Right or Making Money*. 3rd ed. Hoboken, NJ: Wiley,
2014. Kindle.

Desai, Mihir A. *The Wisdom of Finance: Discovering Humanity in the
World of Risk and Return*. Boston: Houghton Mifflin Harcourt, 2017.

Dodonaeus, Rembertus. *Cruydt-Boeck*. 1618 ed. Leiden: Officina
Plantiniana, 1608.

Duke, Annie. *Thinking in Bets: Making Smarter Decisions When You
Don't Have All the Facts*. New York: Portfolio, 2018.

Duvall, James, and Morris Mitler. "Trends in the Expenses and Fees of
Funds, 2017." *ICI Research Perspective* 24, no. 3 (April 2018). Accessed
November 29, 2018. https://www.ici.org/pdf/per24-03.pdf.

Easterling, Ed. "Serious Implications: Forecast Skew over the Next Decade." Crestmont Research. April 6, 2018. Accessed September 18, 2018. https://www.crestmontresearch.com/docs/Stock-Serious -Implications.pdf.

Fama, Eugene F. "Random Walks in Stock Market Prices." *Financial Analysts Journal* 21, no. 5 (September/October 1965): 55–59. doi:10.2469/faj.v21.n5.55.

Fink, Larry. "Larry Fink's 2018 Letter to CEOs: A Sense of Purpose." BlackRock. Accessed January 18, 2019. https://www.blackrock.com/ corporate/investor-relations/2018-larry-fink-ceo-letter.

"Futures Market Basics." U.S. Commodity Futures Trading Commission. Accessed January 26, 2019. https://www.cftc.gov/ ConsumerProtection/EducationCenter/FuturesMarketBasics/index.htm.

Gladwell, Malcom. "Blowing Up." *New Yorker*, April 22, 2002, 162. Accessed September 27, 2018. https://www.newyorker.com/ magazine/2002/04/22/blowing-up.

Goldgar, Anne. *Tulipmania: Money, Honor, and Knowledge in the Dutch Golden Age*. Chicago: University of Chicago Press, 2007. Kindle.

Grable, John E. "Financial Risk Tolerance: A Psychometric Review." *CFA Institute Research Foundation* 4, no. 1 (June 2017): 1–20. doi:10.2470/rfbr.v4.n1.1.

Grantham, Jeremy. "Grantham: Don't Expect P/E Ratios to Collapse." *Barron's*. May 2, 2017. Accessed September 18, 2018. https://www .barrons.com/articles/grantham-dont-expect-p-e-ratios-to-collapse -1493745553.

Grinold, Richard, and Kenneth Kroner. "The Equity Risk Premium." *Investment Insights* 7, no. 2 (July 2002): 7–33. Accessed February 19, 2019. http://www.cfapubs.org/userimages/ ContentEditor/1141674677679/equity_risk_premium.pdf.

Gurdus, Elizabeth. "Lemonis Doubles Down on Long-Term View for Camping World, Says No. 1 Asset Is Loyalty Club." CNBC. September 17, 2018. Accessed February 22, 2019. https://www.cnbc.com/2018/09/17/camping-world-ceo-doubles-down-on-long-term-view-for -retailer.html.

Haque, Umair. *The New Capitalist Manifesto: Building a Disruptively Better Business*. Boston: Harvard Business Review Press, 2011. Kindle.

https://ihsmarkit.com/index.html.

https://www.instituteforsupplymanagement.org.

Hunt, Ben. "Getting Out: A Godfather Story." *Epsilon Theory*. October 27, 2018. Accessed January 15, 2019. https://www.epsilontheory.com/getting-out-a-godfather-story/.

Hunt, Ben. "Things Fall Apart (Part 3)—Markets." *Epsilon Theory*. October 24, 2018. Accessed November 14, 2018. https://www .epsilontheory.com/things-fall-apart-part-3-markets/.

Isidore, Chris, and Blake Ellis. "American Airlines and AMR File for Chapter 11 Bankruptcy." *CNNMoney*. November 29, 2011. Accessed October 2, 2018. https://money.cnn.com/2011/11/29/news/companies/american_airlines_bankruptcy/index.htm.

Johnson, Ben, and Alex Bryan. "Morningstar's Active/Passive Barometer March 2018." Morningstar. March 2018. Accessed January 18, 2019. https://www.morningstar.com/content/dam/marketing/shared/Company/LandingPages/Research/Documents/Morningstar_Active_Passive_Barometer_2018.pdf.

Johnston, Michael. "Ten Shocking ETF Charts from the 'Flash Crash.'" ETF Database. May 7, 2010. Accessed October 3, 2018. http://etfdb.com/2010/ten-shocking-etf-charts-from-the-flash-crash/.

Jones, Kingsley. "Product Design and Financial Literacy." CIFR Paper No. RR/2016. September 21, 2016. doi: 10.2139/ssrn.2842004.

Jung, Jeeman, and Robert J. Shiller. "Samuelson's Dictum and the Stock Market." *Economic Inquiry* 43, no. 2 (April 2005): 221–228. http://www.econ.yale.edu//~shiller/pubs/p1183.pdf.

Kahneman, Daniel, and Amos Tversky. "On the Psychology of Prediction." *Psychological Review* 80, no. 4 (July 1973): 237–251.

Kawa, Luke. "High Frequency Trade: Goldman Warns the Rise of Machines Leaves Markets Exposed." *BloombergQuint*. Last modified May 24, 2018. Accessed October 4, 2018. https://www.bloombergquint .com/markets/goldman-warns-the-rise-of-the-machines-leaves-markets -exposed#gs._1K2qqg.

King, Mervyn A. *The End of Alchemy: Money, Banking, and the Future of the Global Economy*. New York: W. W. Norton & Company, 2016. Kindle.

La Roche, Julia. "Billionaire Hedge Fund Manager Seth Klarman Explains What Makes a Successful Investor." *Business Insider*. January 28, 2016. Accessed January 18, 2019. https://www.businessinsider.com/ seth-klarman-on-what-makes-a-great-investor-2016-1.

La Roche, Julia. "Here Are the Top 20 Hedge Fund Managers of All Time." *Business Insider*. January 26, 2016. Accessed January 18, 2019. https://www.businessinsider.com/top-20-hedge-fund-manager-list -2016-1.

LeGraw, Catherine. "7-Year Asset Class Forecasts Increase After Steep Market Declines." *Advisor Perspectives*. January 16, 2019. Accessed February 19, 2019. https://www.advisorperspectives.com/ commentaries/2019/01/16/7-year-asset-class-forecasts-increase-after -steep-market-declines.

Lewis, Michael. *The Undoing Project: A Friendship That Changed Our Minds*. New York: W. W. Norton & Company, 2017. Kindle.

"Limit Up–Limit Down: Frequently Asked Questions." Nasdaq, 2015. Accessed October 4, 2018. https://www.nasdaqtrader.com/content/MarketRegulation/LULD_FAQ.pdf.

List of supplies published by National Geographic. Accessed October 5, 2016. https://www.nationalgeographic.com/lewisandclark/resources.html (site discontinued).

Lo, Andrew W. *Adaptive Markets: Financial Evolution at the Speed of Thought*. Princeton, NJ: Princeton University Press, 2017. Kindle.

Maillet, Arnaud. "The Claude Glass: Use and Meaning of the Black Mirror in Western Art." Translated by Jeff Fort. Reviewed by Sven Dupré. *Aestimatio 2* (2005): 24-32. http://www.ircps.org/sites/ircps.org/files/aestimatio/2/2005-03-01_Dupre.pdf.

Mandelbrot, Benoit B., and Richard L. Hudson. *The Misbehavior of Markets: A Fractal View of Financial Turbulence*. New York: Basic Books, 2006. Kindle.

Marks, Howard. *Mastering the Market Cycle: Getting the Odds on Your Side*. Boston: Houghton Mifflin Harcourt, 2018. Kindle.

Masturzo, Jim. "Pricing Stocks and Bonds." Research Affiliates. October 2017. Accessed February 19, 2019. https://www.researchaffiliates.com/en_us/publications/articles/641-pricing-stocks-and-bonds.html.

"MSCI ACWI Index (USD)." MSCI. August 31, 2018. Accessed September 26, 2018. https://www.msci.com/documents/10199/a71b65b5-d0ea-4b5c-a709-24b1213bc3c5.

"MSCI ACWI Index (USD)." MSCI. January 31, 2019. Accessed March 4, 2019. https://www.msci.com/documents/10199/a71b65b5-d0ea-4b5c-a709-24b1213bc3c5.

"MSCI Emerging Markets Index (USD)." MSCI. August 31, 2018. Accessed October 1, 2018. https://www.msci.com/documents/10199/c0db0a48-01f2-4ba9-ad01-226fd5678111.

"MSCI USA Index (USD). MSCI." August 31, 2018. Accessed October 1, 2018. https://www.msci.com/documents/10199/67a768a1-71d0 -4bd0-8d7e-f7b53e8d0d9f.

"Mutual Fund Investing Ideas." Fidelity Investments. Accessed November 30, 2018. https://www.fidelity.com/mutual-funds/ investing-ideas/index-funds.

Novick, Barbara, Ananth Madhavan, Samara Cohen, Sal Samandar, Sander Van Nugteren, and Alexis Rosenblum. BlackRock. March 2017. Accessed March 6, 2019. https://www.blackrock.com/corporate/ literature/whitepaper/viewpoint-etf-primary-trading-role-of-authorized -participants-march-2017.pdf.

Ou, Sharon, Sumair Irfan, Yang Liu, Joyce Jiang, and Kumar Kanthan. "Cross-Sector Annual Default Study: Corporate Default and Recovery Rates, 1920–2017." Moody's Investors Service. February 15, 2018. Accessed September 18, 2018. https://www.researchpool.com/ download/?report_id=1751185&show_pdf_data=true.

Pan, Carrie H., and Meir Statman. "Questionnaires of Risk Tolerance, Regret, Overconfidence, and Other Investor Propensities." SCU Leavey School of Business Research Paper No. 10-05. March 10, 2012. doi:10.2139/ssrn.1549912.

Popper, Karl. *The Poverty of Historicism*. London: Routledge, 2002.

Portfolio Charts. Accessed November 20, 2018. https://portfoliocharts .com/.

Poterba, James M., and Andrew A. Samwick. "Stock Ownership Patterns, Stock Market Fluctuations, and Consumption." *Brookings Papers on Economic Activity* 1995, no. 2 (January 1, 1996): 295–372. https://www.brookings.edu/bpea-articles/stock-ownership-patterns -stock-market-fluctuations-and-consumption/.

Randall, Lisa. "Effective Theory. Annual Question 2017: What Scientific Term or Concept Ought to Be More Widely Known?" *Edge*.

2017. Accessed September 17, 2018. https://www.edge.org/response-detail/27044.

Read, Carveth. *Logic, Deductive and Inductive*. 3rd ed. London: Alexander Moring, 1909.

Reichenstein, William, and William Meyer. "Asset Allocation and Asset Location Decisions Revisited." *Journal of Financial Planning* 26, no. 11 (November 2013): 48–55. https://www.onefpa.org/journal/Pages/November-2013-The-Asset-Location-Decision-Revisited.aspx.

Ritholtz, Barry. "MiB: Ned Davis on Risk Management and Mistakes." *The Big Picture*. June 20, 2017. http://ritholtz.com/2017/06/mib-ned-davis-risk-management-mistakes/.

Ritholtz, Barry. "Transcript: Research Affiliates' Rob Arnott." *The Big Picture*. July 29, 2018. Accessed October 17, 2018. https://ritholtz.com/2018/07/transcript-research-affiliates-rob-arnott/.

Ro, Sam. "Jeremy Grantham: The 10 Shakespearean Rules of Investing." *Business Insider*. February 27, 2012. Accessed November 15, 2018. https://www.businessinsider.com/jeremy-grantham-gmo-quarterly-letter-polonius-2012-2#recognize-your-advantages-over-professionals-5.

Robbins, Tony. *Money: Master the Game: 7 Simple Steps to Financial Freedom*. New York: Simon & Schuster, 2014.

"S&P High Yield Dividend Aristocrats." S&P Dow Jones Indices. Accessed October 19, 2018. https://us.spindices.com/indices/strategy/sp-high-yield-dividend-aristocrats-index.

Sandberg, Daniel J. "A Case of 'Wag the Dog'? ETFs and Stock-Level Liquidity." S&P Global. July 2018. Accessed October 3, 2018. https://www.spglobal.com/marketintelligence/en/documents/a-case-of-wag-the-dog-etfs-and-stock-level-liquidity.pdf.

Schnure, Calvin. "Nareit T-Tracker® Results 2018:Q2." Nareit. August 22, 2018. Accessed October 5, 2018. https://www.reit.com/sites/default/files/media/DataResearch/TTracker2018Q2.pdf.

Schoenberger, Chana. "Peter Lynch, 25 Years Later: It's Not Just 'Invest in What You Know.'" *MarketWatch*. December 28, 2015. Accessed September 06, 2018. https://www.marketwatch.com/story/peter-lynch-25-years-later-its-not-just-invest-in-what-you-know-2015-12-28.

Schwartz, David G. "Big Six: A Longitudinal Micro Study." Center for Gaming Research. University Libraries, University of Nevada Las Vegas. 2011.

"SEC Adopts T+2 Settlement Cycle for Securities Transactions." U.S. Securities and Exchange Commission. March 22, 2017. Accessed October 5, 2018. https://www.sec.gov/news/press-release/2017-68-0.

Seiden, Samuel, Steven Albin, and Gaylene Galliford. Computer based trading system and methodology utilizing supply and demand analysis. US Patent 8,650,115. Filed December 20, 2012, and issued February 11, 2014.

Seneca. *Letters from a Stoic: All Three Volumes*. Translated by Richard Mott Gummere. Enhanced Media, 2016. Kindle.

Shiller, Robert. "U.S. Stock Markets 1871–Present and CAPE Ratio." Econ.yale.edu. Last updated May 2019. Accessed May 27, 2019. Excel spreadsheet downloaded at http://www.econ.yale.edu/~shiller/data.htm.

Sloman, Steven, and Philip Fernbach. *The Knowledge Illusion*. New York: Riverhead Books, 2017.

Social Security Administration. "Period Life Table, 2014." Actuarial Life Table. Accessed October 2, 2018. https://www.ssa.gov/OACT/STATS/table4c6.html#fn2.

Soe, Aye M., and Ryan Poirier. "Does Past Performance Matter? The Persistence Scorecard." S&P Dow Jones Indices. January 18, 2018. https://us.spindices.com/documents/spiva/persistence-scorecard-december-2017.pdf.

Soe, Aye M., Berlinda Liu, and Hamish Preston, "SPIVA U.S. Scorecard: Year End 2018," S&P Dow Jones Indices. March 11, 2019.

https://www.spglobal.com/_assets/documents/corporate/us-spiva-report-11-march-2019.pdf.

Solnit, Rebecca. *A Field Guide to Getting Lost*. New York: Viking, 2005. Kindle.

Stein, David. "Should Fiduciaries Overweight Growth Stocks in Investment Portfolios?" Report distributed to clients of Fund Evaluation Group, March, 2000.

Stock price graph for American Airlines Group. Via Google Finance. Accessed October 2, 2018.

Stock price graph for Delta Air Lines. Via Google Finance. Accessed October 2, 2018.

Stock price graph for Southwest Airlines. Via Google Finance. Accessed October 2, 2018.

Stock price graph for United Continental Holdings. Via Google Finance. Accessed October 2, 2018.

Taleb, Nassim Nicholas. *Silent Risk*. Descartes, 2015. Accessed January 15, 2019. http://www.fooledbyrandomness.com/SilentRisk.pdf.

Thole, Herwin. "A 39-Year-Old Who Sold Everything He Owned in Exchange for Bitcoin Now Lives on a Campsite Waiting for the Ultimate Cryptoboom." *Business Insider*. October 10, 2017. Accessed November 15, 2018. https://www.businessinsider.com/man-in-the-netherlands-sold-everything-for-bitcoin-2017-10.

Tuckett, David. "The Role of Emotions in Financial Decisions." Text of the annual Nicholas Barbon Lecture, p. 8. London. May 24, 2012. doi:10.13140/RG.2.1.3777.1921.

Tully, Shawn. "Corporate Profits Are Soaring. Here's Why It Can't Last." *Fortune*. December 7, 2017. Accessed September 18, 2018. http://fortune.com/2017/12/07/corporate-earnings-profit-boom-end/.

Twin, Alexandra. "Stocks Get Pummeled." *CNNMoney*. Last modified September 21, 2008. Accessed September 19, 2018. https://money.cnn .com/2008/09/15/markets/markets_newyork2/.

"US Equity Market Structure: Lessons from August 24." BlackRock. October 7, 2015. Accessed October 3, 2018. https://www.blackrock .com/corporate/literature/whitepaper/viewpoint-us-equity-market -structure-october-2015.pdf.

Vazza, Diane, Nick W. Kraemer, Nivritti Mishra Richhariya, Prachi Bhalla, Abhik Debnath, Praveen Gopinathan, and Aliasger Dohadwala. "Default, Transition, and Recovery: 2016 Annual Global Corporate Default Study and Rating Transitions." Standard & Poor's. April 13, 2017. Accessed September 18, 2018. https://www.spratings.com/ documents/20184/774196/2016+Annual+Global+Corporate +Default+Study+And+Rating+Transitions.pdf/2ddcf9dd-3b82-4151 -9dab-8e3fc70a7035.

Waggoner, John. "John Bogle Says Investors Don't Need to Own International Stocks." *InvestmentNews*. April 29, 2017. Accessed November 15, 2018. https://www.investmentnews.com/article/ 20170429/free/170429919/john-bogle-says-investors-dont-need-to -own-international-stocks.

Watkins, John Elfreth, Jr. "What May Happen in the Next Hundred Years." *Ladies' Home Journal* 18, no. 1 (December 1900).

Webster, Benjamin. "ESG Is Not an Investment Strategy." *Financial Advisor*. May 8, 2017. Accessed January 17, 2019. https://www.fa-mag .com/news/esg-is-not-an-investment-strategy-32655.html.

"Why Are ETFs So Tax Efficient?" ETF.com. Accessed November 30, 2018. https://www.etf.com/etf-education-center/21017-why-are-etfs -transparent-and-tax-efficient.html.

Wigglesworth, Robin. "Global Equity Market Shrinks as Buybacks Surge." *Financial Times*. August 17, 2018. Accessed October 18, 2018. https://www.ft.com/content/5a359796-a18e-11e8-85da-eeb7a9ce36e4.

Wolf, Martin. "Lunch with the FT: Ben Bernanke." *Financial Times*. October 23, 2015. Accessed September 25, 2018. https://www.ft.com/content/0c07ba88-7822-11e5-a95a-27d368e1ddf7.

Xu, Liao, and Xiangkang Yin. "Exchange Traded Funds and Market Volatility: The Case of S&P 500." *SSRN Electronic Journal*, February 11, 2015. doi:10.2139/ssrn.2562704.

Yang, Stephanie. "Oil Hedge Funds Struggle in Age of Algos." *Wall Street Journal*. Last modified June 25, 2018. Accessed September 25, 2018. https://www.wsj.com/articles/how-the-last-commodity-funds-will-survive-the-algo-age-adapt-or-die-1529919003.

Zilbering, Yan, Colleen M. Jaconetti, and Francis M. Kinniry, Jr. "The Buck Stops Here: Vanguard Money Market Funds Best Practices for Portfolio Rebalancing." Vanguard Research. November 2015. Accessed December 4, 2018. https://www.vanguard.com/pdf/ISGPORE.pdf.

Zweig, Jason. "Everyone Makes Investing Mistakes—Even Warren Buffett." *MoneyBeat* (blog). *Wall Street Journal*. June 10, 2018. Accessed September 6, 2018. https://blogs.wsj.com/moneybeat/2018/06/08/everyone-makes-investing-mistakes-even-warren-buffett/.

Notes

Introduction

1. Barry Ritholtz, "MiB: Ned Davis on Risk Management and Mistakes," *The Big Picture*, June 20, 2017, http://ritholtz.com/2017/06/mib-ned-davis -risk-management-mistakes/.
2. Jason Zweig, "Everyone Makes Investing Mistakes—Even Warren Buffett," *MoneyBeat* (blog), Wall Street Journal, June 10, 2018, https://blogs.wsj.com/ moneybeat/2018/06/08/everyone-makes-investing-mistakes-even -warren-buffett/.
3. Annie Duke, *Thinking in Bets: Making Smarter Decisions When You Don't Have All the Facts* (New York: Portfolio, 2018), 27, 33.

Chapter 1

1. Chana Schoenberger, "Peter Lynch, 25 Years Later: It's Not Just 'Invest in What You Know,'" *MarketWatch*, December 28, 2015, https://www .marketwatch.com/story/peter-lynch-25-years-later-its-not-just-invest-in -what-you-know-2015-12-28.
2. Ibid.
3. Elizabeth Gurdus, "Lemonis Doubles Down on Long-Term View for Camping World, Says No. 1 Asset Is Loyalty Club," *Mad Money*, CNBC, September 17, 2018, https://www.cnbc.com/2018/09/17/camping-world -ceo-doubles-down-on-long-term-view-for-retailer.html.
4. James M. Poterba and Andrew A. Samwick, "Stock Ownership Patterns, Stock Market Fluctuations, and Consumption," *Brookings Papers on*

Economic Activity, no. 2 (January 1, 1996): 316, table 6, https://www
.brookings.edu/bpea-articles/stock-ownership-patterns-stock-market
-fluctuations-and-consumption/.

5. Ibid, 317, table 6.
6. Steven Sloman and Philip Fernbach, *The Knowledge Illusion* (New York: Riverhead Books, 2017), 23.
7. Ray Dalio, Introduction to *Principles: Life and Work* (New York: Simon & Schuster, 2017), Kindle.
8. Per Bak, "The Sandpile Paradigm," chap. 3 in *How Nature Works: The Science of Self-Organized Criticality* (New York: Copernicus, 1996).
9. Dalio, Introduction to *Principles: Life and Work*.
10. Dalio, *Principles: Life and Work*, chap. 4.
11. John Elfreth Watkins, Jr., "What May Happen in the Next Hundred Years," *Ladies' Home Journal* 18, no. 1 (December 1900).
12. Ibid.
13. Ned Davis, *Being Right or Making Money*, 3rd ed. (Hoboken, NJ: Wiley, 2014), chap. 1, Kindle.
14. Ibid.
15. Dalio, *Principles: Life and Work*, chap. 4.

Chapter 2

1. Maillet, Arnaud. "The Claude Glass: Use and Meaning of the Black Mirror in Western Art." Translated by Jeff Fort. Reviewed by Sven Dupré. *Aestimatio* 2 (2005): 24-32. http://www.ircps.org/sites/ircps.org/files/aestimatio/2/2005 -03-01_Dupre.pdf.
2. Kingsley Jones, "Product Design and Financial Literacy," CIFR Paper No. RR/2016 (September 21, 2016): 32, doi: 10.2139/ssrn.2842004.
3. Ibid.
4. Anne Goldgar, *Tulipmania: Money, Honor, and Knowledge in the Dutch Golden Age* (Chicago: University of Chicago Press, 2007), Kindle.
5. Rembertus Dodonaeus, *Cruydt-Boeck*, 1618 ed. (Leiden: Officina Plantiniana, 1608), 365.
6. Goldgar, *Tulipmania*, chap. 4, Kindle.
7. "Futures Market Basics," U.S. Commodity Futures Trading Commission, accessed January 26, 2019, https://www.cftc.gov/ConsumerProtection/ EducationCenter/FuturesMarketBasics/index.htm.
8. David G. Schwartz, "Big Six: A Longitudinal Micro Study" (Las Vegas: Center for Gaming Research, University Libraries, University of Nevada Las Vegas, 2011), 1.

9. Jones, "Product Design," 32.
10. "Benefits of Binary Options," Nadex, April 10, 2018, https://www.nadex.com/binary-options/benefits-of-binary-options.
11. Ibid.

Chapter 3

1. E-mail to author, September 3, 2017.
2. Lisa Randall, "Effective Theory—Annual Question 2017: What Scientific Term or Concept Ought to Be More Widely Known?," *Edge*, 2017, https://www.edge.org/response-detail/27044.
3. Ibid.
4. Ibid.
5. Jim Masturzo, "Pricing Stocks and Bonds," Research Affiliates, October 2017, https://www.researchaffiliates.com/en_us/publications/articles/641-pricing-stocks-and-bonds.html; "Capital Market Expectations Methodology Overview," Research Affiliates, revised October 1, 2014, https://www.researchaffiliates.com/documents/AA-Expected-Returns-Methodology.pdf; Richard Grinold and Kenneth Kroner, "The Equity Risk Premium," *Investment Insights* 7, no. 2 (July 2002), https://www.cfapubs.org/userimages/ContentEditor/1141674677679/equity_risk_premium.pdf.
6. Chart B336B, Ned Davis Research, accessed September 20, 2018, https://www.ndr.com/ group/ndr/content-viewer/-/v/ B336B.
7. Charles Barngrover (Emeritus Professor, University of Cincinnati), Intro to Finance class, 1988.
8. Diane Vazza et al., "Default, Transition, and Recovery: 2016 Annual Global Corporate Default Study and Rating Transitions," Standard & Poor's, April 13, 2017, https://www.spratings.com/documents/20184/774196/2016+Annual+Global+Corporate+Default+Study+And+Rating+Transitions.pdf/2ddcf9dd-3b82-4151-9dab-8e3fc70a7035, 20.
9. Sharon Ou et al., "Cross-Sector Annual Default Study: Corporate Default and Recovery Rates, 1920–2017," Moody's Investor Service, February 15, 2018, https://www.researchpool.com/download/?report_id=1751185&show_pdf_data=true.
10. Chart B336B, Ned Davis Research.
11. Masturzo, "Pricing Stocks and Bonds"; Robert Shiller, "U.S. Stock Markets 1871–Present and CAPE Ratio," Econ.yale.edu, last updated May 2019, accessed May 27, 2019, Excel spreadsheet downloaded at http://www.econ.yale.edu/~shiller/data.htm.

12. "Amazon.com, Inc. Revenue & Earnings per Share (EPS)," Nasdaq, accessed March 28, 2019, https://www.nasdaq.com/symbol/amzn/revenue-eps.

13. Ibid.

14. Shawn Tully, "Corporate Profits Are Soaring. Here's Why It Can't Last," *Fortune*, December 7, 2017, http://fortune.com/2017/12/07/corporate -earnings-profit-boom-end/.

15. Ibid.

16. Ed Easterling, "Serious Implications: Forecast Skew over the Next Decade," Crestmont Research, April 6, 2018, https://www.crestmontresearch.com/ docs/Stock-Serious-Implications.pdf, 9, figure 5.

17. Ibid.

18. Jeremy Grantham, "Grantham: Don't Expect P/E Ratios to Collapse," *Barron's*, May 2, 2017, https://www.barrons.com/articles/grantham-dont -expect-p-e-ratios-to-collapse-1493745553.

19. Robin Wigglesworth, "Global Equity Market Shrinks as Buybacks Surge," *Financial Times*, August 17, 2018, https://www.ft.com/content/5a359796 -a18e-11e8-85da-eeb7a9ce36e4.

20. Ibid.

21. William J. Bernstein and Robert D. Arnott, "Earnings Growth: The Two Percent Dilution," *Financial Analysts Journal* 59, no. 5 (September/October 2003): 48, doi:10.2469/faj.v59.n5.2563.

22. https://data.worldbank.org/indicator/NY.GDP.PCAP.KD.ZG.

23. https://interactive.researchaffiliates.com/asset-allocation#!/?currency =USD&model=ER&scale=LINEAR&terms=NOMINAL.

24. Catherine LeGraw, "7-Year Asset Class Forecasts Increase After Steep Market Declines," *Advisor Perspectives*, January 16, 2019, https://www .advisorperspectives.com/commentaries/2019/01/16/7-year-asset-class -forecasts-increase-after-steep-market-declines.

Chapter 4

1. Alexandra Twin, "Stocks Get Pummeled," *CNNMoney*, last modified September 21, 2008, https://money.cnn.com/2008/09/15/markets/markets _newyork2/.

2. Ibid.

3. "MSCI ACWI Index (USD)," MSCI, August 31, 2018, accessed September 26, 2018, https://www.msci.com/documents/10199/a71b65b5-d0ea-4b5c -a709-24b1213bc3c5.

4. "MSCI Emerging Markets Index (USD)," MSCI, August 31, 2018, accessed October 1, 2018, https://www.msci.com/documents/10199/c0db0a48-01f2 -4ba9-ad01-226fd5678111.

5. "MSCI USA Index (USD)," MSCI, August 31, 2018, accessed October 1, 2018, https://www.msci.com/documents/10199/67a768a1-71d0-4bd0 -8d7e-f7b53e8d0d9f.

6. Chart B336B, Ned Davis Research.

7. Peter L. Bernstein, "What Happens If We're Wrong?," *New York Times*, June 22, 2008, https://www.nytimes.com/2008/06/22/business/22view.html? _r=1&oref=slogin&ref=business&pagewanted=print.

8. Ibid.

9. Ibid.

10. John E. Grable, "Financial Risk Tolerance: A Psychometric Review," *CFA Institute Research Foundation* 4, no. 1 (June 2017): 3, doi:10.2470/rfbr .v4.n1.1.

11. Carrie H. Pan and Meir Statman, "Questionnaires of Risk Tolerance, Regret, Overconfidence, and Other Investor Propensities," SCU Leavey School of Business Research Paper, no. 10-05 (March 10, 2012): 1–28, doi:10.2139/ ssrn.1549912.

12. Ibid.

13. Ibid.

14. Daniel Kahneman and Amos Tversky, "On the Psychology of Prediction," *Psychological Review* 80, no. 4 (July 1973): 237.

15. Michael Lewis, *The Undoing Project: A Friendship That Changed Our Minds* (New York: W. W. Norton & Company, 2017), Kindle.

16. Ibid., chap. 7.

17. Ibid., chap. 6.

18. Ibid., chaps. 6, 7.

19. Seneca, *Letters from a Stoic: All Three Volumes*, trans. Richard Mott Gummere (Enhanced Media, 2016), Letter IV, Kindle.

20. Chart T_635.RPT, Ned Davis Research, accessed September 25, 2018, https://www.ndr.com/group/ndr/content-viewer/-/v/T_635*RPT.

21. Mervyn A. King, *The End of Alchemy: Money, Banking, and the Future of the Global Economy* (New York: W. W. Norton & Company, 2016), chap. 4, Kindle.

22. Mihir A. Desai, *The Wisdom of Finance: Discovering Humanity in the World of Risk and Return* (Boston: Houghton Mifflin Harcourt, 2017), 61.

23. Martin Wolf, "Lunch with the FT: Ben Bernanke," *Financial Times*, October 23, 2015, accessed September 25, 2018, https://www.ft.com/content/ 0c07ba88-7822-11e5-a95a-27d368e1ddf7.

24. Ibid.

Chapter 5

1. M. Tullius Cicero, *De Officiis*, trans. Walter Miller (Cambridge, MA: Harvard University Press, 1913), 3.12.50, http://www.perseus.tufts.edu/ hopper/text?doc=Perseus:text:2007.01.0048:book=pos=3:section=50.
2. Ibid.
3. Stephanie Yang, "Oil Hedge Funds Struggle in Age of Algos," *Wall Street Journal*, last modified June 25, 2018, https://www.wsj.com/articles/how-the -last-commodity-funds-will-survive-the-algo-age-adapt-or-die-1529919003.
4. Ibid.
5. Ibid.
6. Samuel Seiden, Steven Albin, and Gaylene Galliford, Computer based trading system and methodology utilizing supply and demand analysis, US Patent 8,650,115, filed December 20, 2012, and issued February 11, 2014.
7. Ibid.
8. Ibid.
9. Ibid.
10. Barry Ritholtz, "Transcript: Research Affiliates' Rob Arnott," *The Big Picture*, July 29, 2018, https://ritholtz.com/2018/07/transcript-research-affiliates -rob-arnott/.
11. Aye M. Soe and Ryan Poirier, "Does Past Performance Matter? The Persistence Scorecard," S&P Dow Jones Indices, January 18, 2018, 1, https://us.spindices.com/documents/spiva/persistence-scorecard-december -2017.pdf.
12. Malcom Gladwell, "Blowing Up,"*New Yorker*, April 22, 2002, 162, https:// www.newyorker.com/magazine/2002/04/22/blowing-up.
13. Aye M. Soe, Berlinda Liu, and Hamish Preston, "SPIVA U.S. Scorecard: Year End 2018," S&P Dow Jones Indices, March 11, 2019 https:// www.spglobal.com/_assets/documents/corporate/us-spiva-report-11-march -2019.pdf.
14. Ben Johnson and Alex Bryan, "Morningstar's Active/Passive Barometer March 2018," Morningstar, March 2018, https://www.morningstar.com/ content/dam/marketing/shared/Company/LandingPages/Research/ Documents/Morningstar_Active_Passive_Barometer_2018.pdf.
15. Ritholtz, "Transcript: Research Affiliates' Rob Arnott."
16. Soe and Poirier, "Does Past Performance Matter?"
17. Eugene F. Fama, "Random Walks in Stock Market Prices," *Financial Analysts Journal* 21, no. 5 (September/October 1965): 56, doi:10.2469/faj.v21 .n5.55.
18. Andrew Ang, *Asset Management: A Systematic Approach to Factor Investing* (Oxford: Oxford University Press, 2014).

19. Jeeman Jung and Robert J. Shiller, "Samuelson's Dictum and the Stock Market," *Economic Inquiry* 43, no. 2 (April 2005): 221, http://www.econ .yale.edu//~shiller/pubs/p1183.pdf.
20. David Stein, "Should Fiduciaries Overweight Growth Stocks in Investment Portfolios?" (report distributed to clients of Fund Evaluation Group, March 2000): 4.
21. Andrew W. Lo, *Adaptive Markets: Financial Evolution at the Speed of Thought* (Princeton, NJ: Princeton University Press, 2017), chap. 6, Kindle.
22. Ibid., chaps. 2, 4.
23. Ibid., chap. 6.
24. Lo, Introduction to *Adaptive Markets*.
25. David Tuckett, "The Role of Emotions in Financial Decisions" (text of the annual Nicholas Barbon Lecture, London, May 24, 2012), p. 8, doi:10.13140/RG.2.1.3777.1921.
26. Lo, *Adaptive Markets*, chap. 8.
27. Ray Dalio, *Principles: Life and Work* (New York: Simon & Schuster, 2017), chap. 4. Kindle.

Chapter 6

1. Chris Isidore and Blake Ellis, "American Airlines and AMR File for Chapter 11 Bankruptcy," *CNNMoney*, November 29, 2011, https://money.cnn.com/ 2011/11/29/news/companies/american_airlines_bankruptcy/index.htm.
2. Stock price graph for American Airlines Group, via Google Finance, accessed October 2, 2018; stock price graph for Delta Air Lines, via Google Finance, accessed October 2, 2018; stock price graph for Southwest Airlines, via Google Finance, accessed October 2, 2018; stock price graph for United Continental Holdings, via Google Finance, accessed October 2, 2018.
3. American Airlines stock.
4. Social Security Administration, "Period Life Table, 2014," Actuarial Life Table, accessed October 2, 2018, https://www.ssa.gov/OACT/STATS/ table4c6.html#fn2.
5. "SEC Adopts T+2 Settlement Cycle for Securities Transactions," U.S. Securities and Exchange Commission, March 22, 2017, https://www.sec .gov/news/press-release/2017-68-0.
6. Calvin Schnure, "Nareit T-Tracker° Results 2018: Q2," Nareit, August 22, 2018, 12, https://www.reit.com/sites/default/files/media/DataResearch/ TTracker2018Q2.pdf.
7. As filed with the Securities and Exchange Commission on August 13, 2018, Offering Circular Fundrise Equity REIT, LLC.

8. "Average Premium/Discount" widget, Closed-End Fund Association, accessed October 5, 2018, http://www.cefa.com.

9. "Closed-End Funds Daily Pricing," CEF Connect, accessed October 5, 2018, https://www.cefconnect.com/closed-end-funds-daily-pricing.

10. *2018 Investment Company Fact Book: A Review of Trends and Activities in the Investment Company Industry*, 58th ed. (Washington, DC: Investment Company Institute, 2018), 2017 Facts at a Glance, https://www.ici.org/pdf/2018_factbook.pdf.

11. Barbara Novick et al., "A Primer on ETF Primary Trading and the Role of Authorized Participants," BlackRock, March 2017, 3, exhibit 2, https://www.blackrock.com/corporate/literature/whitepaper/viewpoint-etf-primary-trading-role-of-authorized-participants-march-2017.pdf.

12. Liao Xu and Xiangkang Yin, "Exchange Traded Funds and Market Volatility: The Case of S&P 500," *SSRN Electronic Journal*, February 11, 2015, doi:10.2139/ssrn.2562704; Itzhak Ben-David, Francesco A. Franzoni, and Rabih Moussawi, "Do ETFs Increase Volatility?," Fisher College of Business WP 2011-03-20, December 2, 2011, last revised November, 2017, doi:10.2139/ssrn.1967599.

13. Daniel J. Sandberg, "A Case of 'Wag the Dog'? ETFs and Stock-Level Liquidity," S&P Global, July 2018, 2, https://www.spglobal.com/marketintelligence/en/documents/a-case-of-wag-the-dog-etfs-and-stock-level-liquidity.pdf.

14. "Limit Up–Limit Down: Frequently Asked Questions," Nasdaq, 2015, 1, accessed October 4, 2018, https://www.nasdaqtrader.com/content/MarketRegulation/LULD_FAQ.pdf.

15. "US Equity Market Structure: Lessons from August 24," BlackRock, October 7, 2015, 1–3, https://www.blackrock.com/corporate/literature/whitepaper/viewpoint-us-equity-market-structure-october-2015.pdf.

16. Ibid., 3; Michael Johnston, "Ten Shocking ETF Charts from the 'Flash Crash,'" ETF Database, May 7, 2010, http://etfdb.com/2010/ten-shocking-etf-charts-from-the-flash-crash/.

17. "US Equity Market Structure: Lessons from August 24," 3.

18. Ibid.

19. Ibid., 5–6.

20. Luke Kawa, "High Frequency Trade: Goldman Warns the Rise of Machines Leaves Markets Exposed," *BloombergQuint*, May 24, 2018, https://www.bloombergquint.com/markets/goldman-warns-the-rise-of-the-machines-leaves-markets-exposed#gs._1K2qqg.

21. Ibid.

Chapter 7

1. Martin Wolf, "Lunch with the FT: Ben Bernanke," *Financial Times*, October 23, 2015, accessed September 25, 2018, https://www.ft.com/content/0c07ba88-7822-11e5-a95a-27d368e1ddf7.

2. Rebecca Solnit, *A Field Guide to Getting Lost* (New York: Viking, 2005), Open Door, Kindle.

3. Annie Duke, *Thinking in Bets: Making Smarter Decisions When You Don't Have All the Facts* (New York: Portfolio, 2018), 27, 33.

4. List of supplies published by *National Geographic*, accessed October 5, 2016, https://www.nationalgeographic.com/lewisandclark/resources.html (site discontinued).

5. Carveth Read, *Logic, Deductive and Inductive*, 3rd ed. (London: Alexander Moring, 1909), 320.

6. Howard Marks, *Mastering the Market Cycle: Getting the Odds on Your Side* (Boston: Houghton Mifflin Harcourt, 2018), Cycle Positioning, Kindle.

7. E-mail messages to author, October 11–15, 2018.

8. Rob Arnott, Shane Shepherd, and Bradford Cornell, "Yes. It's a Bubble. So What?," Research Affiliates, April 2018, https://www.researchaffiliates.com/en_us/publications/articles/668-yes-its-a-bubble-so-what.html.

9. E-mail messages to author, October 11–15, 2018.

10. Ibid.

11. Ibid.

12. Chart S09, Ned Davis Research, accessed October 19, 2018, https://www.ndr.com/group/ndr/content-viewer/-/v/S09.

13. Ibid.

14. "S&P High Yield Dividend Aristocrats," S&P Dow Jones Indices, accessed October 19, 2018, https://us.spindices.com/indices/strategy/sp-high-yield-dividend-aristocrats-index.

15. Andrew Ang, *Asset Management: A Systematic Approach to Factor Investing*. (Oxford: Oxford University Press, 2014).

16. Rob Arnott et al., "How Can 'Smart Beta' Go Horribly Wrong?," Research Affiliates, February 2016, https://www.researchaffiliates.com/en_us/publications/articles/442_how_can_smart_beta_go_horribly_wrong.html.

17. Rob Arnott, Vitali Kalesnik, and Lillian Wu, "The Incredible Shrinking Factor Return," Research Affiliates, April 2017, https://www.researchaffiliates.com/documents/601-The Incredible Shrinking Factor Return.pdf?mod=article_inline.

18. Howard Marks, *The Most Important Thing: Uncommon Sense for the Thoughtful Investor* (New York: Columbia University Press, 2011), chap. 25, Kindle.

19. Bendix Anderson, "Investment Sales Slowdown Hits the Student Housing Sector," *National Real Estate Investor*, July 17, 2017, https://www.nreionline .com/student-housing/investment-sales-slowdown-hits-student-housing -sector.

Chapter 8

1. E-mail message to author, August 29, 2018.
2. James Duvall, "Trends in the Expenses and Fees of Funds, 2018," *ICI Research Perspective* 25, no. 1 (March 2019): 1, https://www.ici.org/pdf/ per25-01.pdf.
3. "Mutual Fund Investing Ideas," Fidelity Investments, accessed November 30, 2018, https://www.fidelity.com/mutual-funds/investing-ideas/index-funds.
4. "Why Are ETFs So Tax Efficient?," ETF.com, accessed November 30, 2018, https://www.etf.com/etf-education-center/21017-why-are-etfs-transparent -and-tax-efficient.html.
5. William Reichenstein and William Meyer, "Asset Allocation and Asset Location Decisions Revisited," *Journal of Financial Planning* 26, no. 11 (November 2013): 48–55, https://www.onefpa.org/journal/Pages/November -2013-The-Asset-Location-Decision-Revisited.aspx.
6. Yan Zilbering, Colleen M. Jaconetti, and Francis M. Kinniry, Jr., "The Buck Stops Here: Vanguard Money Market Funds Best Practices for Portfolio Rebalancing," Vanguard Research, November 2015, 12, https:// www.vanguard.com/pdf/ISGPORE.pdf.

Chapter 9

1. Benoit B. Mandelbrot and Richard L. Hudson, *The Misbehavior of Markets: A Fractal View of Financial Turbulence* (New York: Basic Books, 2006), chap. 5, Kindle.
2. Nassim Nicholas Taleb, *Silent Risk* (Descartes, 2015), http://www .fooledbyrandomness.com/SilentRisk.pdf, iii.
3. Ben Hunt, "Things Fall Apart (Part 3)—Markets," *Epsilon Theory*, October 24, 2018, https://www.epsilontheory.com/things-fall-apart-part-3-markets/.
4. Ben Hunt, "Getting Out: A Godfather Story," *Epsilon Theory*, October 27, 2018, https://www.epsilontheory.com/getting-out-a-godfather-story/.
5. David Tuckett, "The Role of Emotions in Financial Decisions" (text of the annual Nicholas Barbon Lecture, London, May 24, 2012), p. 8, doi:10.13140/RG.2.1.3777.1921.
6. Herwin Thole, "A 39-Year-Old Who Sold Everything He Owned in Exchange for Bitcoin Now Lives on a Campsite Waiting for the Ultimate

Cryptoboom," *Business Insider*, October 10, 2017, https://www
.businessinsider.com/man-in-the-netherlands-sold-everything-for-bitcoin
-2017-10; David Tuckett, "The Role of Emotions in Financial Decisions"
(text of the annual Nicholas Barbon Lecture, London, May 24, 2012), p. 8,
doi:10.13140/RG.2.1.3777.1921.

7. Mervyn A. King, *The End of Alchemy: Money, Banking, and the Future of the Global Economy* (New York: W. W. Norton & Company, 2016), chap. 4, Kindle.

8. MSCI Emerging Markets Index (USD), MSCI, August 31, 2018, accessed October 1, 2018, https://www.msci.com/documents/10199/c0db0a48-01f2 -4ba9-ad01-226fd5678111.

9. Sam Ro, "Jeremy Grantham: The 10 Shakespearean Rules of Investing," *Business Insider*, February 27, 2012, https://www.businessinsider.com/ jeremy-grantham-gmo-quarterly-letter-polonius-2012-2#recognize-your -advantages-over-professionals-5.

10. John Waggoner, "John Bogle Says Investors Don't Need to Own International Stocks," *InvestmentNews*, April 29, 2017, https://www.investmentnews.com/ article/20170429/free/170429919/john-bogle-says-investors-dont-need-to -own-international-stocks.

11. "Apple Inc. (AAPL) Stock Report," Nasdaq, accessed November 8, 2018, https://www.nasdaq.com/symbol/aapl/stock-report.

12. MSCI ACWI Index (USD), January 31, 2019.

13. Barry Ritholtz, "Transcript: Research Affiliates' Rob Arnott," *The Big Picture*, July 29, 2018, https://ritholtz.com/2018/07/transcript-research-affiliates -rob-arnott/.

14. Tony Robbins, *Money: Master the Game: 7 Simple Steps to Financial Freedom* (New York: Simon & Schuster, 2014), chap. 5.1, Kindle.

15. Portfolio Charts, accessed November 20, 2018, https://portfoliocharts.com/.

Chapter 10

1. Chart T_635.RPT, Ned Davis Research, accessed September 25, 2018, https://www.ndr.com/group/ndr/content-viewer/-/v/T_635*RPT.

2. https://ihsmarkit.com/index.html; https://www.instituteforsupplymanagement .org.

3. Chart S1102, Ned Davis Research, accessed September 20, 2018, https:// www.ndr.com/group/ndr/content-viewer/-/v/S1102.

4. Benjamin Webster, "ESG Is Not an Investment Strategy," *Financial Advisor*, May 8, 2017, accessed January 17, 2019, https://www.fa-mag.com/news/ esg-is-not-an-investment-strategy-32655.html.

5. Larry Fink, "Larry Fink's 2018 Letter to CEOs: A Sense of Purpose," BlackRock, accessed January 18, 2019, https://www.blackrock.com/ corporate/investor-relations/2018-larry-fink-ceo-letter.

6. Umair Haque, *The New Capitalist Manifesto: Building a Disruptively Better Business* (Boston: Harvard Business Review Press, 2011), chap. 1, Kindle.

7. Karl Popper, *The Poverty of Historicism* (London: Routledge, 2002), 61.

8. Ibid.

Conclusion

1. Julia La Roche, "Here Are the Top 20 Hedge Fund Managers of All Time," *Business Insider*, January 26, 2016, https://www.businessinsider.com/top-20 -hedge-fund-manager-list-2016-1.

2. Julia La Roche, "Billionaire Hedge Fund Manager Seth Klarman Explains What Makes a Successful Investor," *Business Insider*, January 28, 2016, https://www.businessinsider.com/seth-klarman-on-what-makes-a-great -investor-2016-1.

3. Andrew W. Lo, *Adaptive Markets: Financial Evolution at the Speed of Thought* (Princeton, NJ: Princeton University Press, 2017), chap. 6, Kindle.

Index

About the Author

J. DAVID STEIN helps individuals become better and more confident investors through his writing, audio, and video. David hosts the personal finance podcast *Money For the Rest of Us*. The show has over 10 million downloads and reaches more than 40,000 listeners per episode. David also provides investment insights and model portfolios to 1,000 members of the Money For the Rest of Us Plus community. Prior to launching the podcast over five years ago, David advised and managed assets for institutions and financial planners. He was Chief Investment Strategist and Chief Portfolio Strategist at Fund Evaluation Group, LLC, a $70 billion investment advisory firm, where he coheaded the 21-person research group. He cofounded the firm's $2.2 billion asset management division where he developed its investment philosophy and process and was the lead portfolio manager. David perfected his teaching style as an investment consultant to numerous not-for-profit institutions where he assisted the boards and staff in overseeing billions of dollars in endowment assets. David splits his time between Idaho, Arizona, and locations around the globe. In his free time, he loves to hike, fly-fish, bike, read, and spend time with his family.